Table of Contents

Introduction

Types of Stories
- fairy tales
- folktales

Ways to Use the Stories
1. Directed lessons
   - with small groups of students who are reading at the same level
   - with an individual student
   - with the class to support a unit of study

2. Partner reading

3. With cooperative learning groups

4. Independent practice
   - at school
   - at home

Things to Consider
1. Determine your purpose for selecting a story—instructional device, partner reading, group work, or independent reading. Each purpose calls for a different degree of story difficulty.

2. A single story may be used for more than one purpose. You might first use the story as an instructional tool, have partners read the story a second time for greater fluency, and then use the story at a later time for independent reading.

3. When presenting a story to a group or an individual for the first time, review any vocabulary that will be difficult to decode or understand. Many students will benefit from a review of the vocabulary page and the questions before they read the story.

2

Types of Skill Pages

Three or four pages of activities covering a variety of reading skills follow each story:

- comprehension
- vocabulary
- phonics
- structural analysis
- parts of speech
- categorizing

Ways to Use Skill Pages

1. Individualize skill practice for each student with tasks that are appropriate for his or her needs.

2. As directed minilessons, the skill pages may be used in several ways:
   - Make a transparency for students to follow as you work through the lesson.
   - Write the activity on the board and call on students to fill in the answers.
   - Reproduce the page for everyone to use as you direct the lesson.

3. When using the skill pages for independent practice, make sure that the skills have been introduced to the reader. Review the directions and check for understanding. Review the completed lesson with the students to determine if further practice is needed.

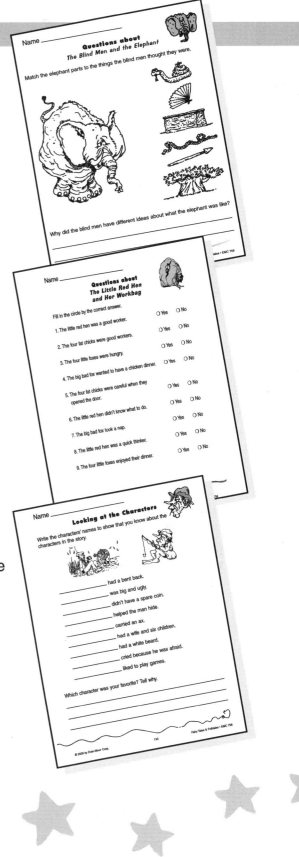

So Quiet!

The house was so loud. The boys were yelling. The girls were crying. Father was pounding. Mother sat down. "I can't do my work," she said. "It is too loud!"

She went to see Grandpa. "Grandpa, my house is too loud. The boys are yelling. The girls are crying. Father is pounding. What can I do?"

Grandpa looked up. "No problem," he said. "Bring the dog and the cat into the house."

Mother walked home. She called the dog and the cat into the house. The boys were yelling. The girls were crying. Father was pounding. And the dog was barking at the cat. Mother sat down. "I can't do my work," she said. "It is too loud!"

She went back to Grandpa. "Grandpa, my house is louder. The boys are still yelling. The girls are still crying. Father is still pounding. And now the dog is barking at the cat. What can I do?"

Grandpa nodded. "No problem," he said. "Bring the rooster and the cow into the house."

Mother walked home. She pulled the cow and the rooster into the house. The boys were yelling. The girls were crying. Father was pounding. The dog was barking at the cat. The cow was mooing. And the rooster was crowing. Mother sat down. "I can't do my work," she said. "It is too loud!"

She went back to Grandpa. "Grandpa, my house is louder. The boys are still yelling. The girls are still crying. Father is still pounding. The dog is still barking at the cat. Now the cow is mooing and the rooster is crowing. What can I do?"

Grandpa smiled. "No problem," he said. "The cat and the dog and the cow and the rooster must go back outside."

Mother walked back home. She took the cow, the rooster, the dog, and the cat outside. The boys were still yelling. The girls were still crying. Father was still pounding. Mother smiled. "Now I can do my work! It is so quiet."

Fairy Tales & Folktales • EMC 756

Name _____

Questions about
So Quiet!

Fill in the correct circle.

1. Mother couldn't
   ○ go to sleep   ○ hear the TV   ○ do her work

2. She went to see
   ○ Grandpa   ○ Grandma   ○ Uncle Pete

3. Grandpa always said,
   ○ "How can I help you?"   ○ "Please come in."   ○ "No problem!"

4. First Grandpa made the house
   ○ louder   ○ quieter   ○ bigger

5. When all the animals went outside, the house was
   ○ louder   ○ quieter   ○ bigger

6. At the end the house sounded _____ at the beginning.
   ○ louder than   ○ quieter than   ○ the same as

bang woof boom moo bang meow woof moo bang

Name _____

What Comes Next?

Color, cut, and paste. Put the pictures in order.

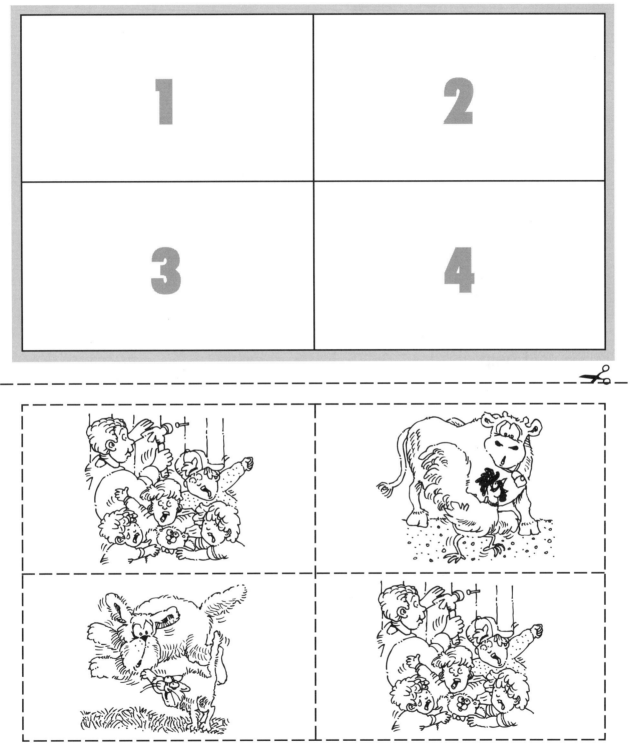

1	**2**
3	**4**

meow · bang · woof · boom · moo · bang · meow · woof · moo

7   Fairy Tales & Folktales • EMC 756

Name _____

Quiet Work and Loud Work

Think about things people do that are loud and things that are quiet. Write or draw them below.

Loud	Quiet

bang woof boom moo bang meow woof moo bang

Name _____

The Sound of *qu*

Color the pictures that begin with the sound that **qu** makes.

How many did you find? _____

May I Come In?

Miss Annie lived in a tiny hut. She had room for her broom, her cooking pot, and her bed.

One day a cute kitten purred by her door. "May I come in?" the kitten asked. "It is cold and I am hungry."

Miss Annie looked at the sad kitten. Her head said, "No, you don't have much room." Her heart said, "Yes! Yes! Yes!" Miss Annie let the kitten in.

Miss Annie and the kitten were happy in the hut. There was just room for the cooking pot and the bed.

One day a woolly goat butted her door. "May I come in?" the goat asked. "It is cold and I am hungry."

Miss Annie looked at the sad goat. Her head said, "You don't have much room." Her heart said, "Yes! Yes! Yes!" Miss Annie let the goat in.

Miss Annie, the kitten, and the goat were happy in the hut. There was just room for the bed.

One day a sleepy bear pawed at her door. "May I come in?" the bear asked. "It is cold and I am sleepy."

Miss Annie looked at the sad bear. Her head said, "You don't have much room." Her heart said, "Yes! Yes! Yes!" Miss Annie let the bear in.

Miss Annie, the kitten, the goat, and the bear were happy in the hut. There was no more room.

One day a tiny mouse squeaked at her door. "May I come in?" the mouse asked. "It is cold and I need a home."

Miss Annie looked at the sad mouse. She looked at the kitten, the goat, and the bear. Her head said, "You don't have room." Her heart said, "Yes! Yes! Yes! It's only a little mouse." Miss Annie let the mouse in.

This time Miss Annie's head was right. The tiny mouse squeezed into the house. The house rocked from side to side. It creaked. It groaned. It exploded! Miss Annie, the kitten, the goat, the bear, and the mouse were blown high into the sky.

Fairy Tales & Folktales • EMC 756

Name _____

Questions about
May I Come In?

Draw in the boxes to show what fit in the house.

In the beginning…

Next…

Then…

What happened when the tiny mouse moved in?

_____

Name _____

Will It Fit?

Draw a bed that will fit

in a wagon.	in a truck.

Draw a kitten that will fit

in a cup.	in a basket.

Draw a bear that will fit

in a car.	in a bowl.

ly I Come In? May I Come In? May I Come In?

13   Fairy Tales & Folktales • EMC 756

Rhyme Time

Color, cut, and paste to show rhyming pairs.

Come In? 🏠 May I Come In? 🏠 May I Come In? 🏠 Ma

Name _____

Working with Word Families
-oom

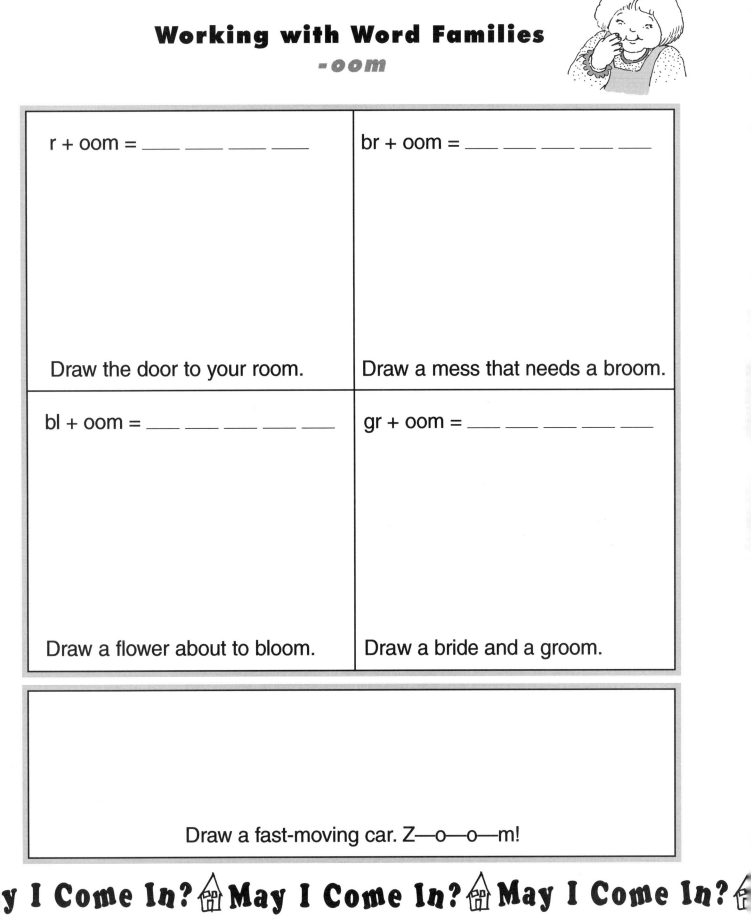

r + oom = ___ ___ ___ ___

Draw the door to your room.

br + oom = ___ ___ ___ ___

Draw a mess that needs a broom.

bl + oom = ___ ___ ___ ___ ___

Draw a flower about to bloom.

gr + oom = ___ ___ ___ ___

Draw a bride and a groom.

Draw a fast-moving car. Z—o—o—m!

y I Come In? May I Come In? May I Come In?

15   Fairy Tales & Folktales • EMC 756

The Blind Men and the Elephant

Once there were six blind men who went to see an elephant.

The first blind man put his hands in front of himself. He felt the elephant's huge side. "This elephant is like a high, strong wall."

The second man was standing near the elephant's head. He put his hands on its long tusk. "A wall? No! I would say it is more like a spear."

The third man reached around the elephant's leg. "I think that you're both wrong. An elephant is like a strong tree."

The fourth man happened to reach out and touch the elephant's ear. "It seems to me that the elephant is like a giant fan."

The fifth man was standing by himself at the elephant's other end. He grabbed the elephant's tail. "A wall? A spear? A tree? A fan? No, an elephant is like a rope."

The elephant reached out. It touched the sixth man with his trunk. The man jumped and pushed the trunk away. "Friends, move back! The elephant is really a very large snake."

The six men left the elephant quickly. Each felt he knew what an elephant was like.

Name _____

Questions about
The Blind Men and the Elephant

Match the elephant parts to the things the blind men thought they were.

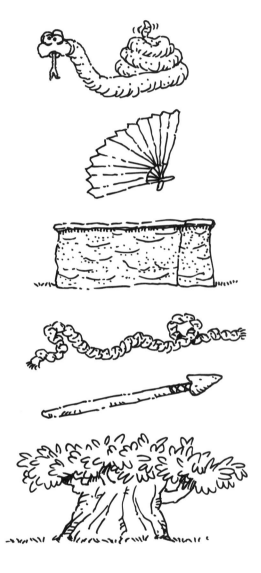

Why did the blind men have different ideas about what the elephant was like?

_____

_____

18   Fairy Tales & Folktales • EMC 756

Name _____

First, Second, Third

Write the ordinal numbers below on the correct lines.

Word Box				
first	third	fifth	seventh	ninth
second	fourth	sixth	eighth	tenth

_____

_____

_____

_____

_____

_____

_____

_____

_____

Fairy Tales & Folktales • EMC 756

Name _____

Working with Word Families
-ind

f + ind = ___ ___ ___ ___   w + ind = ___ ___ ___ ___

k + ind = ___ ___ ___ ___   bl + ind = ___ ___ ___ ___ ___

m + ind = ___ ___ ___ ___   gr + ind = ___ ___ ___ ___ ___

Use the words you made to complete these sentences.

1. How many eggs can you _____?

2. _____ the toy car to make it go.

3. The _____ man had a special dog.

4. It was _____ of you to help.

5. _____ your grandma.

6. _____ means to cut into little bits.

                                       Fairy Tales & Folktales • EMC 756

Name _____

The Sound of f

Color the pictures that have the sound that **f** makes.
Circle the word that tells where you hear the sound.

beginning   middle   end

beginning   middle   end

beginning   middle   end

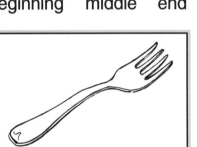

beginning   middle   end

beginning   middle   end

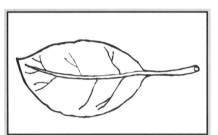

beginning   middle   end

●●● ph Says f ●●●

The two letters **ph** work together. They make the same sound as **f**.

phone

Fill in the letters to name the pictures.

ele ___ ___ ant

___ ___ oto

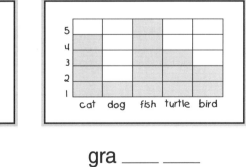

gra ___ ___

Teeny-Tiny

There was a teeny-tiny woman. She lived in a teeny-tiny house in a teeny-tiny town. One day the teeny-tiny woman went for a teeny-tiny stroll. She buttoned her teeny-tiny coat. She put on her teeny-tiny hat. She opened her teeny-tiny door. She walked down the teeny-tiny path.

She came to a teeny-tiny gate. The teeny-tiny woman opened the teeny-tiny gate. She walked into a teeny-tiny churchyard. She saw a teeny-tiny bone on top of a teeny-tiny grave. The teeny-tiny woman said, "Look! A teeny-tiny bone! A teeny-tiny treat for my teeny-tiny dog." The teeny-tiny woman took the teeny-tiny bone from the teeny-tiny grave. She put the teeny-tiny bone into her teeny-tiny pocket. Then the teeny-tiny woman went back to her teeny-tiny house.

When the teeny-tiny woman got home, she was a teeny-tiny sleepy. She climbed into her teeny-tiny bed. The teeny-tiny woman closed her teeny-tiny eyes for a teeny-tiny nap. Then she heard a teeny-tiny voice. The voice said, "Give me my bone!"

Fairy Tales & Folktales • EMC 756

The teeny-tiny woman was a teeny-tiny bit scared. She hid her teeny-tiny head under her teeny-tiny quilt. She went to sleep again. When she had been asleep for a teeny-tiny time, the voice woke her again. It was a teeny-tiny bit louder.

"Give me my bone!"

The teeny-tiny woman was a teeny-tiny bit more scared. She hid her teeny-tiny head a teeny-tiny bit farther under the quilt. In a teeny-tiny time, the teeny-tiny woman heard the voice again. It was a teeny-tiny louder.

"Give me my bone!"

By now the teeny-tiny woman was a teeny-tiny bit more scared. She took her head out from under her teeny-tiny quilt and said in her loudest teeny-tiny voice:

"TAKE IT!"

Fairy Tales & Folktales • EMC 756

Name _____

Questions about
Teeny-Tiny

1. Where did the teeny-tiny woman live.

_____

_____

2. Tell three things the teeny-tiny woman did before her teeny-tiny stroll.

_____

_____

_____

3. What did the teeny-tiny woman find?

_____

_____

4. Why did the teeny-tiny woman take the teeny-tiny bone?

_____

_____

5. Did the teeny-tiny dog get the bone?

_____

_____

Name _____

What Happened Next?

Number the pictures to tell the order of the story.

Name _____

Adding *er*

Add **er** to the words. Draw to show what the new word means.

loud	louder

loud + er = ____ ____ ____ ____ ____ ____

tall	taller

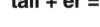

tall + er = ____ ____ ____ ____ ____ ____

soft	softer

soft + er = ____ ____ ____ ____ ____ ____

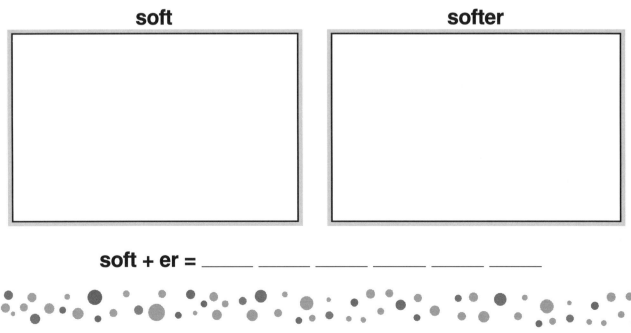

Name _____

Opposites

Color, cut, and paste. Sort the pictures to show which things are teeny-tiny and which things are great big.

These things are teeny-tiny.   These things are great big.

| paste | paste | | paste | paste |

| paste | paste | | paste | paste |

27   Fairy Tales & Folktales • EMC 756

The Old Woman and Her Pig

An old woman went for a walk with her pig. She came to a big puddle in the road. Her pig jumped into the puddle. The pig wouldn't move.

So the old woman went on. She saw a dog. She said to the dog, "Dog, Dog, bite the pig. Pig won't move out of the puddle and I can't go home." The dog just stood by the road.

So the old woman went on. She saw a stick. She said to the stick, "Stick, Stick, beat the dog. Dog won't bite the pig. Pig won't move out of the puddle. And I can't go home." The stick just lay in the road.

So the old woman went on. She saw a fire. She said to the fire, "Fire, Fire, burn the stick. Stick won't beat the dog. Dog won't bite the pig. Pig won't move out of the puddle. And I can't go home." The fire just burned by the road.

So the old woman went on. She saw some water. She said to the water, "Water, Water, put out the fire. Fire won't burn the stick. Stick won't beat the dog. Dog won't bite the pig. Pig won't move out of the puddle. And I can't go home." The water just stood by the road.

So the old woman went on. She saw a horse. She said to the horse, "Horse, Horse, drink the water. Water won't put out the fire. Fire won't burn the stick. Stick won't beat the dog. Dog won't bite the pig. Pig won't move out of the puddle. And I can't go home." The horse just flicked his tail.

So the old woman went on. She saw a horsefly. She said to the horsefly, "Horsefly, Horsefly, sting the horse. Horse won't drink the water. Water won't put out the fire. Fire won't burn the stick. Stick won't beat the dog. Dog won't bite the pig. Pig won't move out of the puddle. And I can't go home." The horsefly just buzzed.

So the old woman went on. She saw a boy. She said to the boy, "Boy, Boy, swat the horsefly. Horsefly won't sting the horse. Horse won't drink the water. Water won't put out the fire. Fire won't burn the stick. Stick won't beat the dog. Dog won't bite the pig. Pig won't move out of the puddle. And I can't go home." The boy said, "Get me a branch. I will swat the horsefly."

So the old woman went to a bush. She pulled off a branch. She took the branch to the boy. The boy began to swat the horsefly. The horsefly began to sting the horse. The horse began to drink the water. The water began to put out the fire. The fire began to burn the stick. The stick began to beat the dog. The dog began to bite the pig. The muddy pig jumped out of the puddle and ran all the way home.

Name _____

Questions about
The Old Woman and Her Pig

1. Who did the old woman take on her walk?
   - ○ her dog
   - ○ her cow
   - ○ her pig

2. What was the old woman's problem?
   - ○ She was tired.
   - ○ Her pig wouldn't move.
   - ○ She got lost.

3. What caused the problem?
   - ○ a fire
   - ○ a horsefly
   - ○ a puddle

4. Why do you think the pig jumped into the puddle?
   - ○ It was thirsty.
   - ○ It was mad.
   - ○ It was hot.

Fill in the blanks to tell the order.

The _____ began to swat the _____.

The _____ began to sting the _____.

The _____ began to drink the _____.

The _____ began to put out the _____.

The _____ began to burn the _____.

The _____ began to beat the _____.

The _____ began to bite the _____.

The _____ jumped out of the puddle and ran home.

31   Fairy Tales & Folktales • EMC 756

Name _____

Making Sentences

Cut and paste. Create sentences that make good sense.
Draw a picture for each sentence.

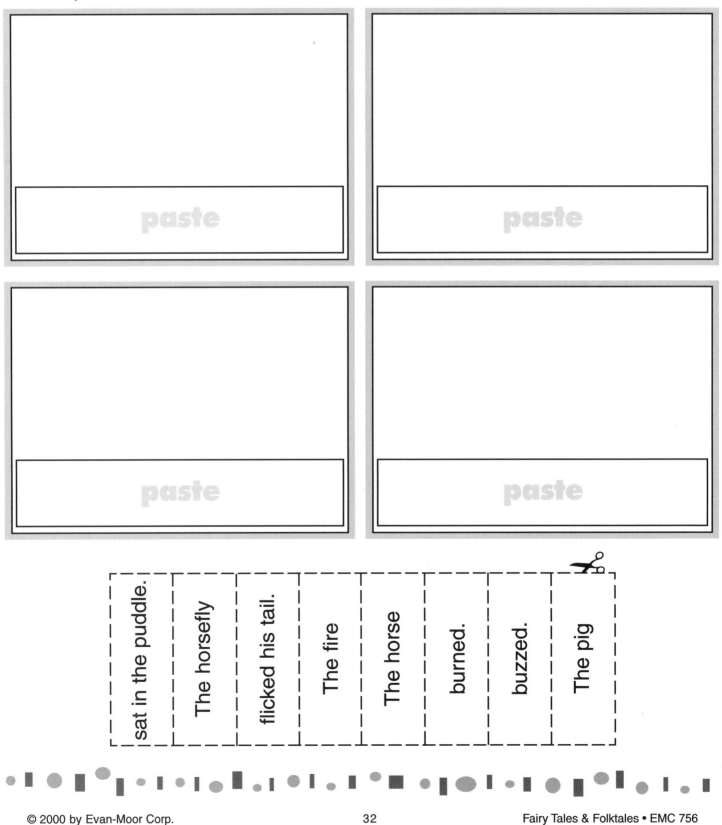

paste	paste
paste	paste

sat in the puddle. The horsefly flicked his tail. The fire The horse burned. buzzed. The pig

Name _____

Working with Word Families
-uddle

h + uddle = ___ ___ ___ ___ ___ ___

m + uddle = ___ ___ ___ ___ ___ ___

p + uddle = ___ ___ ___ ___ ___ ___

c + uddle = ___ ___ ___ ___ ___ ___

Use the new words in these sentences.

1. She walked in the _____ that the rain made.

2. The football team made a _____.

3. My kitten loves to _____.

4. Mrs. Smith's desk is in a _____.

Draw what your room would look like if it was in a muddle.

The Three Sticks

An Iroquois Tale

Two boys were arguing. Each thought that he was right. Each boy put up a fist and shook it at the other.

Then the boys' mother gave them three sticks. She explained, "These are special sticks. They will solve your argument."

The mother walked into the woods with her sons. Each carried a stick. When they had gone a little way they stopped. "Now we set up the sticks," she said. She showed the boys how to lean the three sticks together so that they stood alone.

Then she said, "The sticks must be left for one month. If they fall over toward the north, the one who set up the stick on the north is right. If they fall over to the south, the one who set up the stick on the south is right." The boys were happy. They left the sticks in the woods and went home.

A month later, the boys thought of the sticks. They went into the woods to find out who had been right. The sticks had fallen in a heap. They had begun to rot. There was no winner. The boys didn't mind. They couldn't remember what the argument had been about in the first place.

Name _____

Questions about
The Three Sticks

1. What was the problem?

_____

_____

2. How was the problem solved?

_____

_____

3. Who was the winner?

_____

_____

4. Why didn't the boys mind?

_____

_____

5. Write one way you would solve a problem.

_____

_____

Name _____

What Does It Mean?

Match each word to its meaning.

argument   a pile

explain   by oneself

alone   a fight

heap   to tell about

Use the words above in these sentences.

1. The two girls had an _____.

2. They threw the coats in a _____.

3. Each one sat _____.

4. It was hard to _____ what happened.

Draw something you do alone.

                                       Fairy Tales & Folktales • EMC 756

Name _____

Long e

Two **e**'s together in a word usually have the long sound
of **e** that you hear in **three**.

Draw to show what would make each sound.

cheep   beep   tweet   gee

Crossword Puzzle

Complete this puzzle using
ee words.

Across
1. blue + yellow = _____
3. to look
4. a forest animal

Down
2. The boys _____ help.
5. The _____ Sticks

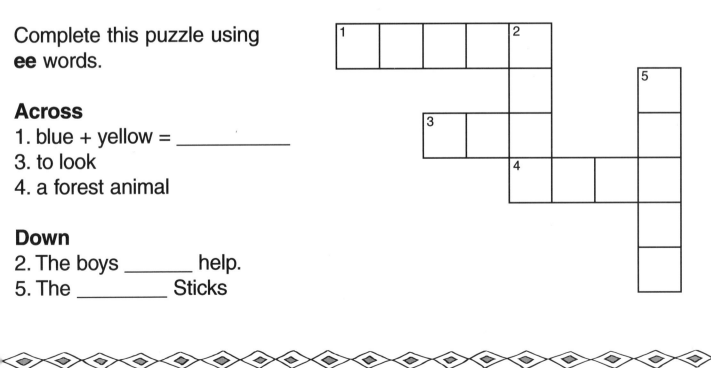

Name _____

The Sounds of *oi–oy*

The letters **oi** and **oy** make the same sound.
    oy is used at the end of a word   **boy**
    oi is used at the beginning or in the middle   **oi**l   s**oi**l

Write the missing letters in these words.

t ____ ____   j ____ ____   b ____ ____   c ____ ____ n

j ____ ____ n   n ____ ____ se   p ____ ____ nt   sp ____ ____ l

Color, cut, and paste to put the story pictures in order.
Use some of the words above to complete the story.

paste	paste	paste
He wants a gum ball. See him _____.	He puts a _____ in the slot.	Wow! He gets a _____.

The Biggest Pumpkin

A Tale from Africa

Do you know why there are so many stars? It all started with a very big pumpkin...

There was once a big pumpkin. It was so big that the people called it Feegba. Feegba was a good name. It means "big thing." Never had a pumpkin grown so big. It was as tall as a man. It was as round as the full moon. It was as orange as the bright sun. It was the biggest and best pumpkin ever to grow in Africa.

One day a farmer came to harvest the pumpkin. He had a large knife. He started to cut the pumpkin open.

"Ouch!" cried the pumpkin. "Stop cutting me! That hurts!"

"No," said the farmer. "I will cook you. We will have a feast. All the people will be happy. Their stomachs will be full."

"Eating me is not a good thing!" said the pumpkin. "Take your knife and go away!"

Fairy Tales & Folktales • EMC 756

"You are ripe," said the man. "We must eat you before you spoil." The man sliced the stem with his knife.

"Now I am angry!" said the pumpkin. "I do not want to be eaten!"

Slowly, the pumpkin began to roll toward the man. The man backed away. The pumpkin rolled faster and faster. The man ran away. The pumpkin rolled faster and faster like a huge rolling pin. It smashed into a small hill and rolled it flat. It squashed a hut. It knocked down trees. The man ran for his life.

At last the man came to a jagged rock. He fell down in a heap behind it. The pumpkin couldn't slow down. It hit the rock with a loud thud! It split open. The pumpkin seeds flew up into the sky. They became shining stars.

And the man with the knife? For as long as he lived, he never cut open a pumpkin again.

Name _____

Questions about
The Biggest Pumpkin

1. Who were the two characters in the story?

_____   _____

2. What did the farmer do to the pumpkin?

_____

_____

3. How did the pumpkin feel?

_____

_____

4. What happened to the pumpkin?

_____

_____

5. The tale told how a group of things came to be. What are the things?

_____

_____

6. Why didn't the man ever cut open a pumpkin again?

_____

_____

Name _____

Silent *k*

When you read **kn**, the **k** does not make a sound. You say just the sound of **n**.

knock   **kn**ow

Each of the pictures below is a **kn** word. Write the picture names on the lines.

Word Box		
doorknob	knife	knee
knapsack	knot	knight

_____   _____   _____

_____   _____   _____

Write a sentence using one of the **kn** words.

_____

_____

                   Fairy Tales & Folktales • EMC 756

Name _____

The Sound of e

Color the pictures that have the same vowel sound as **seed**.

Name _____

Faster, Faster

Read all the boxes before you begin.

Draw a **fast** car.

Draw a **faster** car.

Draw a **fast** animal.

Draw a **faster** animal.

Draw a **fast** worker.

Write to tell how the worker could be **faster**.

_____

_____

_____

_____

Fairy Tales & Folktales • EMC 756

Chicken Licken

One day Chicken Licken walked down the road. An acorn fell on her head. "Help! The sky is falling!" she said. "I must go to tell the king."

So she ran along the road. She met her friend, Henny Penny. "Henny Penny, the sky is falling!" said Chicken Licken.

"How do you know?" asked Henny Penny.

"A piece fell on my head," Chicken Licken answered. "I must go to tell the king. Come with me."

So Chicken Licken and Henny Penny went off down the road. They met their friend, Cocky Locky. "Cocky Locky, the sky is falling! The sky is falling!"

"How do you know?" asked Cocky Locky.

"A piece fell on my head," Chicken Licken answered. "We are going to tell the king. Come with us."

So Chicken Licken, Henny Penny, and Cocky Locky went off down the road. They met their friend, Turkey Lurkey. "Turkey Lurkey, the sky is falling! The sky is falling!"

"How do you know?" asked Turkey Lurkey.

"A piece fell on my head," Chicken Licken answered. "We are going to tell the king. Come with us."

So Chicken Licken, Henny Penny, Cocky Locky, and Turkey Lurkey went off down the road. They met their friend, Goosey Loosey. "Goosey Loosey, the sky is falling! The sky is falling!"

"How do you know?" asked Goosey Loosey.

"A piece fell on my head," Chicken Licken answered. "We are going to tell the king. Come with us."

So Chicken Licken, Henny Penny, Cocky Locky, Turkey Lurkey, and Goosey Loosey went off down the road. They met Foxy Loxy. "Foxy Loxy, the sky is falling! The sky is falling!" said Chicken Licken.

"How do you know?" asked Foxy Loxy.

"A piece fell on my head," Chicken Licken answered. "We are going to tell the king. Come with us."

"Wait!" said Foxy Loxy licking his chops. "If the sky is falling, you will not be safe. Come to my den. It is safe there."

So Chicken Licken, Henny Penny, Cocky Locky, Turkey Lurkey, and Goosey Loosey went with Foxy Loxy to his den. Foxy Loxy ate them all, every one.

Name _____

Questions about
Chicken Licken

1. What did Chicken Licken think was happening?

_____

_____

2. What did each animal ask Chicken Licken?

_____

_____

3. What did Chicken Licken answer?

_____

_____

4. Did Foxy Loxy think the sky was falling?   Yes   No
   Tell why you think as you do.

_____

_____

_____

_____

Name _____

Rhyme Time

Each of the animals in the story has a name that rhymes.

Chicken Licken   Goosey Loosey   Foxy Loxy

Write a rhyming name for each of these animals.

Tiger _____   Kitten _____   Puppy _____

Hamster _____   Monkey _____   Bunny _____

Which character in the story has a **different** rhyming name than the others?

_____

Name _____

Using an Exclamation Mark

A sentence that "shouts" something needs an **exclamation mark** at the end.

The sky is falling! The sky is falling!

Read each sentence. Decide if the sentence needs an exclamation mark.
Put a period or an exclamation mark at the end of each sentence.
Draw a picture to show what is happening.

Chicken Licken walked down the road

We are going to tell the king

Help The sky is falling

Wait Come to my den

Name _____

The Letter *y* Can Say *i*

The letter **y** at the end of a word sometimes has the **i** sound you hear in **sky**.

Start with **sky**.

1. Take off **sk** and add **sl**.   ___ ___ ___

   The fox is _____.

2. Take off **sl** and add **fl**.   ___ ___ ___

   Airplanes and birds _____.

3. Take off **fl** and add **cr**.   ___ ___ ___

   Please don't _____!

4. Take off **cr** and add **wh**.   ___ ___ ___

   _____ is the sun hot?

5. Take off **wh** and add **dr**.   ___ ___ ___

   The towel is _____.

6. Take off **dr** and add **fr**.   ___ ___ ___

   Will you _____ the egg?

The Magic Pot

A mother and her son sat by their hut. They felt as empty as hollow logs. They worked hard. They were good and honest. But they did not have food to keep their stomachs full.

One day, as the boy chopped wood, he met a funny little man. The man saw that the boy was hungry. He felt sorry for the boy and gave him a magic pot. The man showed the boy how to use the pot. When the pot heard the words, "Cook, Magic Pot, cook!" it filled itself with tasty soup. When it heard, "Stop, Magic Pot, stop!" it stopped.

The boy took the pot home. He made tasty soup for his mother. They ate and ate. They were as full as sausages stuffed for market. Each day the boy and his mother worked hard. Then they ate the tasty soup the boy made with the pot.

One day the boy took a load of wood to a nearby town. While he was gone, his mother got hungry. She had watched her son cook soup with the magic pot. She decided to cook some soup for herself. She put the pot in the middle of the table. She said, "Cook, Magic Pot, cook!"

The magic pot bubbled. It was filled with tasty soup. The woman ate and ate and ate. The magic pot kept bubbling. The woman did not remember the words to make the pot stop.

Fairy Tales & Folktales • EMC 756

The soup spilled over the edge of the pot. The pot kept bubbling. The soup spilled off the table. The pot kept bubbling. The soup spilled out the door. The pot kept bubbling. The soup ran down the road. The pot kept bubbling.

On his way home from the town, the boy saw a river of soup running down the road. He jumped out of the way. He sloshed along the edge of the road. He ran into his house. He yelled, "Stop, Magic Pot, stop!"

The pot stopped. The last of the soup ran out the door. From that day on, the boy carried his pot with him wherever he went. His mother never again tried to use magic that she didn't understand.

Name _____

Questions about
The Magic Pot

Write numbers to show the order in which things happened in the story.

_____ The funny little man gave the boy a magic pot.

_____ The mother and boy were stuffed.

_____ The boy made soup.

_____ The mother and son were hungry.

_____ The mother never used magic to make soup again.

_____ The soup spilled out the door.

_____ The boy was chopping wood.

_____ The mother made soup.

_____ The boy told the pot to stop.

Do you like soup?   yes   no

What is your favorite kind?

_____

53

Name _____

Working with Word Families
-ook

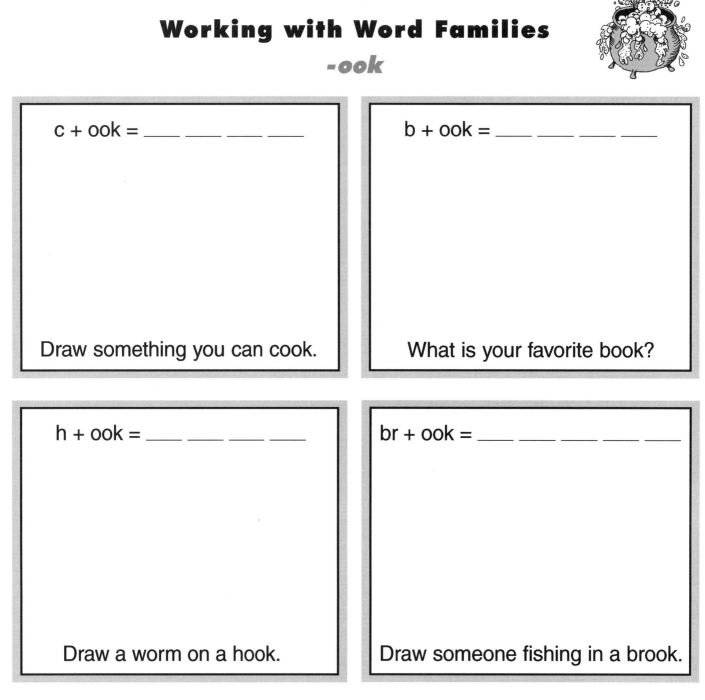

c + ook = ___ ___ ___ ___

Draw something you can cook.

b + ook = ___ ___ ___ ___

What is your favorite book?

h + ook = ___ ___ ___ ___

Draw a worm on a hook.

br + ook = ___ ___ ___ ___

Draw someone fishing in a brook.

Use one of the **-ook** words to complete these compound words.

fish_____

note_____

Fairy Tales & Folktales • EMC 756

Rhyme Time

Color, cut, and paste to show rhyming pairs.

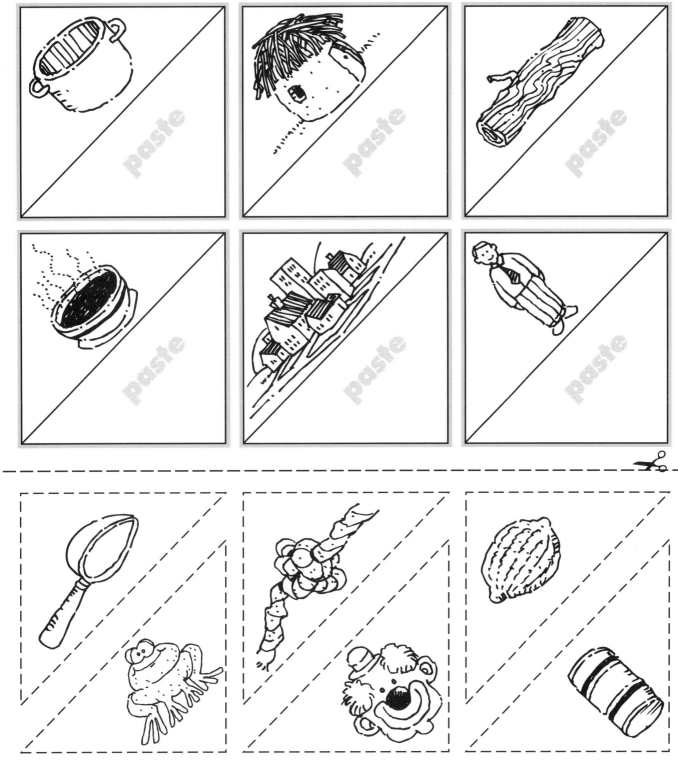

Name _____

Different Meanings

Sometimes one word can have many different meanings.
Draw to show the different meanings of **stuffed**.

I have a **stuffed** animal.

The butcher **stuffed** the sausage.

After supper I was **stuffed**.

Draw something you
have that is **stuffed**.

The Pied Piper of Hamlin

A Tale from the Grimm Brothers

In the town of Hamlin there were too many rats. There were rats in the homes. There were rats in the shops. There were rats in the schools. There were rats in the streets. The townsfolk tried to get rid of the rats. Nothing they did worked. Instead of fewer rats, there were more rats.

The mayor of Hamlin called a meeting. "We must get rid of the rats. Let us offer a reward!"

The townsfolk cheered, "What a good idea!" So the news went out. Anyone who could get rid of the rats would get a bag of gold.

Soon a stranger came to town. He was dressed in bright colors. When he walked he seemed to dance. He went straight to the mayor's house. "I have come to rid your town of rats," he told the mayor.

The mayor laughed, "You are welcome to try. Many have failed. I don't think you will be able to do it."

The stranger nodded, "Think as you may. You will soon see. But when the job is done, I want the gold."

"Do the job and you shall have it," said the mayor.

The stranger took a wooden pipe from his belt. He put the pipe to his mouth. He started to play. The rats on the street pricked up their ears. They ran to the sound. The rats in the homes pricked up their ears. They ran to the sound. The rats in the shops pricked up their ears. They ran to the sound. The rats in the schools pricked up their ears. They ran to the sound. Soon all the rats in the town were following the stranger. They followed him out of town. They followed him down the road. The stranger led them to the edge of the river. The rats jumped in and drowned.

There were no rats left in Hamlin. The townsfolk cheered. "What a good job you did!" they told the piper.

"Thank you," said the piper. "Now I would like my gold."

The mayor frowned. "A bag of gold is too great a reward for such an easy task," he said. "All you did was play a tune."

The townsfolk looked at each other. They were sorry they had offered a bag of gold. They nodded and said, "Yes, it was a simple job. You only played a tune. You should not get a bag of gold."

The piper turned. "You will pay in one way or another," he said. He put the pipe to his lips. He played another tune. This time the children of the town ran to the piper. They ran from their homes. They ran from the shops. They ran from the schools. They ran from the streets. The children followed the piper out of town and down the road. And the townsfolk never saw their children again.

Name _____

Questions about
The Pied Piper of Hamlin

1. What was the problem?

_____

2. How did the town solve the problem?

_____

3. What did the stranger look like?

_____

_____

4. How did the stranger get rid of the rats?

_____

_____

5. Why didn't the mayor give the stranger the reward?

_____

_____

6. What did the stranger mean when he said, "You will pay one way or another"?

_____

_____

 Fairy Tales & Folktales • EMC 756

Name _____

The Sounds of ow-ou

Sometimes the letters **ow** and **ou** make the sound you hear in **town**.

Circle the words that have that sound.

mouth	follow	town	down
house	your	out	now
could	sound	drown	you

Use the words above to complete these sentences.

1. The _____ of Hamlin had a problem.

2. The piper put his pipe to his _____.

3. The rats were in every _____.

4. The piper said, "_____ I will make the rats follow me."

5. The rats will _____.

6. Have you ever heard the pipe's _____?

Name _____

Crossword Puzzle

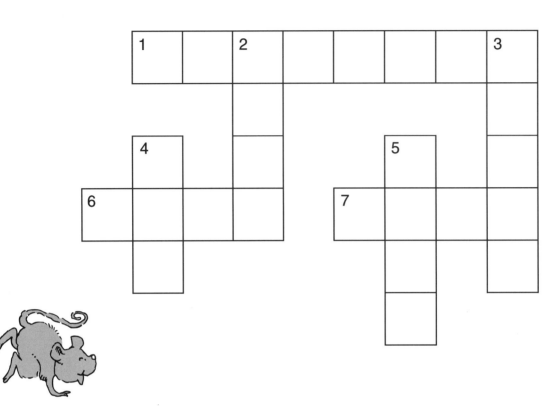

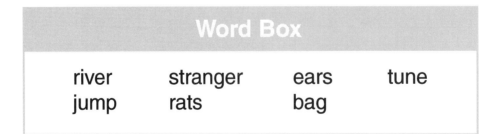

Across
1. someone you don't know
6. you hear with them
7. a little song

Down
2. like big mice
3. a stream of water
4. a sack
5. to leap

Word Box

river	stranger	ears	tune
jump	rats	bag	

Fairy Tales & Folktales • EMC 756

The Little Red Hen and Her Workbag

Once there was a little red hen. She had four fat chicks. A big bad fox and four little foxes lived close by.

One morning the little foxes said, "Father, we are hungry. We have nothing to eat."

The big bad fox shook his head. He thought and thought. Then he said, "I will catch a nice fat hen and four nice fat chicks! I will bring them back for your supper."

The four little foxes jumped for joy. The big bad fox took his sack and went on his way.

Now that same morning, the four fat chicks got up on the wrong side of the bed. One chick said that the day was too hot. One chick said that the day was too cold. But when they walked into the kitchen, the little red hen was cheerful.

"Who will get some sticks to light the fire?" she asked.

"I won't," said one chick.

"I won't," said another chick.

"And we won't either!" said the other two chicks.

"Then I will do it myself," said the little red hen. And off she went to get the sticks.

When she came back, she asked, "Who will fill the pot?"

"I won't," said one chick.

"I won't," said another.

"And we won't either!" said the other two chicks.

"Then I will do it myself," said the little red hen. And she filled the pot.

So the day went. The little red hen was busy and cheerful as she worked. The four fat chicks were napping. The big bad fox knocked at the door.

The four chicks jumped up. "Who could it be?" Then without looking to see who it was, they ran to the door. As soon as the door was opened, the big bad fox jumped in. "Help! Help!" cried the four fat chicks.

The fox caught the chicks. He popped them into his sack. The little red hen came running. The fox caught her, too, and put her into the sack with the chicks. He took a piece of string out of his pocket. He tied up the mouth of the sack. Then he threw the sack over his back.

The four fat chicks started to cry. "Don't be so sad," whispered the little red hen. "I have my workbag. Be quiet. Wait and see what I will do."

The sun was very hot. The sack was very heavy. The big bad fox stopped to rest under a tree. He fell asleep. The little red hen opened her workbag. She took out her scissors. She snipped a hole in the sack. "Quick!" she said to the chicks. "Run as fast as you can. Bring back stones to put in the sack."

So the four chicks ran. They came back with stones. They pushed them into the sack. The little red hen took out her needle and thread. She quickly sewed up the hole. Then the little red hen and her four chicks ran home. They slammed the door and locked it tight.

Not long after, the big bad fox woke up. He picked up the heavy sack and went home. He got the cooking pot ready. But when he opened the sack, there were only stones inside. So the four little foxes had to go to bed without any supper.

     Fairy Tales & Folktales • EMC 756

Name _____

Questions about
The Little Red Hen
and Her Workbag

Fill in the circle by the correct answer.

1. The little red hen was a good worker. ○ Yes ○ No

2. The four fat chicks were good workers. ○ Yes ○ No

3. The four little foxes were hungry. ○ Yes ○ No

4. The big bad fox wanted to have a chicken dinner. ○ Yes ○ No

5. The four fat chicks were careful when they
   opened the door. ○ Yes ○ No

6. The little red hen didn't know what to do. ○ Yes ○ No

7. The big bad fox took a nap. ○ Yes ○ No

8. The little red hen was a quick thinker. ○ Yes ○ No

9. The four little foxes enjoyed their dinner. ○ Yes ○ No

Name _____

Adding Endings

Add the endings to the words.

	ed	**ing**
fill	_____	_____
work	_____	_____
knock	_____	_____
open	_____	_____
sew	_____	_____

Add the final letter and the endings.

	ed	**ing**
nap	_____	_____
stop	_____	_____
slam	_____	_____

Fill in the missing words.

1. The little red hen _____ hard.

2. The four fat chicks _____.

3. The big bad fox _____ on the door.

4. The four fat chicks _____ the door.

5. The big bad fox _____ the sack with his dinner.

Name _____

Getting Up on the Wrong Side of the Bed

When someone is grumpy and things go wrong in the morning, we sometimes say that person **got up on the wrong side of the bed**.

Mark Yes or No.

Tom got up on the wrong side of the bed.

Yes   No

Tonya got up on the wrong side of the bed.

Yes   No

Father got up on the wrong side of the bed.

Yes   No

Draw what might happen if you got up on the wrong side of the bed.

The Ugly Duckling

A Tale from Hans Christian Andersen

Mother Duck sat on her nest. There were six eggs there—five smooth white eggs and one big gray egg. Mother Duck waited for her eggs to hatch.

One day the five smooth white eggs cracked. Out popped five soft yellow ducklings. The big gray egg didn't crack. Mother Duck waited for the last egg to hatch. Finally the big egg cracked. Out crawled a big gray duckling with a long neck. The five soft yellow ducklings crowded around. "You are not one of us!" they said. "You are ugly."

The new baby was very sad. Mother Duck tried to protect the big gray duckling. But the other ducklings pecked at it. They chased it away.

The lonely duckling made a home by the marsh. The wild ducks and the geese lived there. They left the duckling alone. It paddled through the marsh looking for food.

Many days went by. Fall came. The leaves on the trees turned red. They fell to the ground. The air was cold. The gray duckling watched a flock of snow-white birds with long necks fly over the marsh. The flock was going south for the winter. The duckling cried, "If only I could be one of those pretty birds."

Fall turned to winter. The ugly duckling was cold. The marsh was frozen. The duckling hid in the woods. It was cold and hungry. The long winter passed slowly.

Finally the days became warmer. The marsh thawed. It had been a year since the ugly duckling had hatched. It found its way back to the marsh. Sadly, it began swimming all alone.

On the other side of the marsh were two of the white birds with the long necks. They had returned. The white birds swam toward the duckling. It was afraid. Were they going to peck it? Would they chase it from the marsh? The birds stretched their necks toward the duckling. They touched it gently. The duckling was happy.

Then the ugly duckling looked down into the water. It was amazed. It didn't see an ugly gray baby. It saw a snow-white bird with a long neck. It was beautiful!

The ugly gray duckling had become a graceful white swan. It swam proudly in the marsh with the other swans.

Name _____

Questions about
The Ugly Duckling

Choose the best answer.

1. Mother Duck was

   ○ patient   ○ lazy   ○ tired

2. The smooth white eggs cracked

   ○ too soon   ○ before the big egg   ○ after the big egg

3. The yellow ducklings chased the big gray duckling because

   ○ it was different   ○ they were older
   ○ they liked to play tag

4. The big gray duckling wished that

   ○ it was summer   ○ it was a graceful swan
   ○ its mother liked it

5. The big gray duckling became

   ○ a beautiful swan   ○ a mean bully   ○ just like the others

6. Was Mother Duck a good mother? Explain your answer.

   _____

   _____

   _____

Name _____

Animal Babies

Color, cut, and paste to match the parents with their babies.

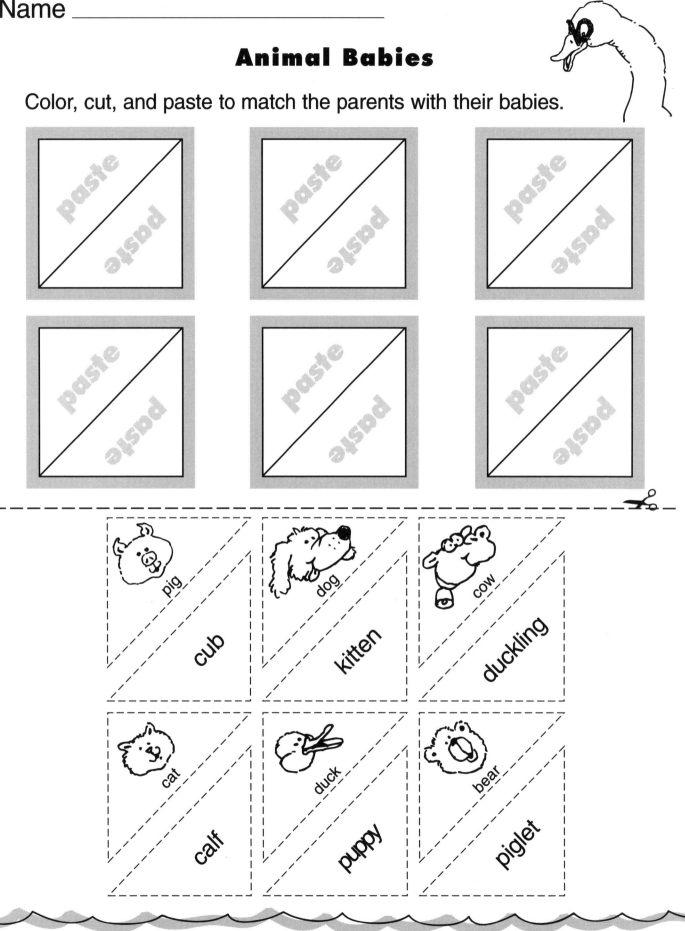

Name _____

Working with Word Families
-atch

c + atch = ____ ____ ____ ____ ____   l + atch = ____ ____ ____ ____ ____

h + atch = ____ ____ ____ ____ ____   m + atch = ____ ____ ____ ____ ____

b + atch = ____ ____ ____ ____ ____   p + atch = ____ ____ ____ ____ ____

Draw a picture to show what happens.

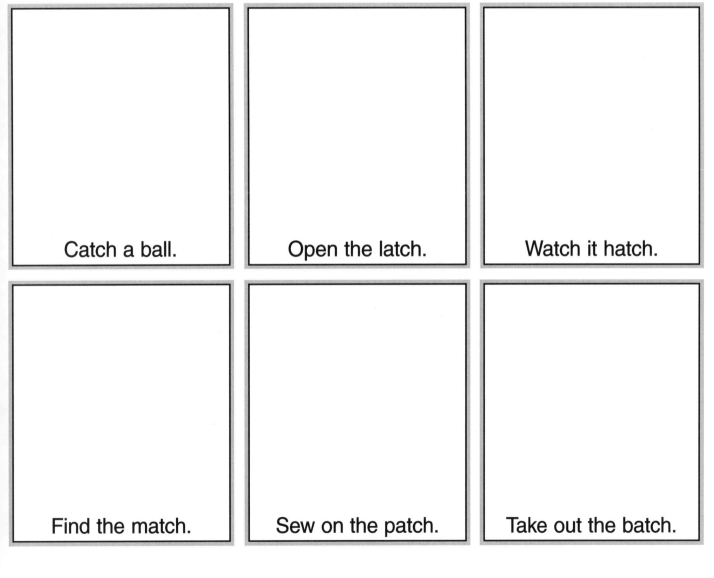

Catch a ball.

Open the latch.

Watch it hatch.

Find the match.

Sew on the patch.

Take out the batch.

Name _____

The Lesson

The Ugly Duckling is a story with a moral or a lesson.
What lesson does this story teach?

_____

_____

Write or draw to show what that lesson means to you.

What a Fool!

Once there was a girl named Rose. Each day she watched her father work. She wanted to help, but she didn't know how. Rose's father worked hard. He didn't take the time to teach Rose.

One day he sent Rose to the market. Rose carried a bag of wheat to sell. She sold it for a penny. But Rose lost the penny on the way home.

"What a fool!" said her father. "You should have put it in your pocket."

"OK, I'll do that next time," said Rose.

The next day Rose's father asked Rose to get a bucket of milk. Rose went to the dairy. She got a bucket of milk. She poured it into her pocket. It ran out as she walked. It was all gone when she got home.

"What a fool!" said her father. "You should have carried it on your head."

"OK, I'll do that next time," said Rose.

Fairy Tales & Folktales • EMC 756

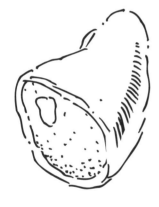

The next day Rose went to the store for cheese. She took the cheese. She put it on her head. Then she walked home. The sun was hot. The cheese melted.

"What a fool!" said her father. "You should have carried it in your hands."

"OK, I'll do that next time," said Rose.

The next day Rose found a big rooster. She wanted to take the rooster home. Rose took it carefully in her hands. Before long the rooster had scratched her so badly that she had to let it go.

When Rose got home, her father said, "What a fool!" You should have tied it with a string and pulled it home."

"OK, I'll do that next time," said Rose.

The next day Rose went to the butcher for ham. Rose took the ham, tied it to a string, and pulled it behind her. She pulled it in the dirt. By the time she got home, the ham was not fit to eat. Rose's father was hungry. His meat was ruined.

"What a fool!" he said. "You should have carried it on your shoulder."

"OK, I'll do that next time," said Rose.

The next day Rose wanted to help again. Her father asked her to use the wheelbarrow to move the firewood into the barn. Rose thought about what he had said. The wheelbarrow was heavy. But Rose hoisted it onto her shoulder. She began to walk to the barn.

A rich and handsome king saw Rose. He stopped and asked what she was doing. Rose told the king that she wanted to help her father. She told him about the penny and the milk and the cheese and the rooster and the ham and the wheelbarrow. The king listened carefully. Then he said, "What a fool your father is! Come with me. You have a good heart, but an empty head. My daughter will teach you how to do things. And you can show her how to work hard."

"OK," said Rose. And so Rose went to live with the king and his daughter. She learned how to do many things and lived a happy life.

Name _____

Questions about
What a Fool!

1. What was Rose's problem?

_____

_____

_____

2. What did Rose's father always say to her?

_____

_____

_____

3. What did Rose always say?

_____

_____

_____

4. Who was the biggest fool in the story? Tell why.

_____

_____

_____

_____

The Best Way

Help Rose find the best way to carry things. Draw a good way to carry
each of these things. Write a sentence to tell how.

_____   _____

_____   _____

_____   _____

_____   _____

Name _____

Working with Word Families
-each

b + each = ___ ___ ___ ___ ___   t + each = ___ ___ ___ ___ ___

p + each = ___ ___ ___ ___ ___   r + each = ___ ___ ___ ___ ___

bl + each = ___ ___ ___ ___ ___ ___   pr + each = ___ ___ ___ ___ ___ ___

Use the **-each** words above to complete these sentences.
Draw a picture to show what each sentence means.

My mother used _____ to get my shirt white.	I love _____ ice cream.
I cannot _____ the book.	Let's go to the _____.

                                       Fairy Tales & Folktales • EMC 756

The Three Little Pigs

One day three little pigs left home. They walked along the road together. Soon they met a man with a wagon full of straw. The first little pig had an idea. "Please, Sir, may I have some of your straw?" The man gave the pig some straw and went on his way. The first little pig used the straw to build a house.

The two other little pigs walked on. Soon they met a man with a cart full of sticks. The second little pig had an idea. "Please, Sir, may I have some of your sticks?" The man gave the pig some sticks and went on his way. The second little pig used the sticks to build a house.

The third little pig walked on. He met a man with a load of bricks. The third little pig had an idea. "Please, Sir, may I have some of your bricks?" The man gave the pig some bricks and went on his way. The third little pig used the bricks to build a house.

Not far away there lived a hungry wolf. The wolf saw the first little pig's house of straw. He wanted Little Pig for lunch. He walked up to the straw house. He tapped on the door. *Tap, tap, tap.* "Little Pig, Little Pig, let me come in."

The pig saw the wolf and said, "Not by the hair on my chinny-chin-chin."

The hungry wolf was mad. He shouted, "Then I'll huff and I'll puff and I'll blow your house in!" And the wolf huffed and he puffed and he blew the house in. Little Pig ran to the second pig's stick house.

The mad, hungry wolf followed the pig. He saw the house of sticks. He walked up to the door. *Tap, tap, tap.* "Little Pigs, Little Pigs, let me come in." The wolf's mouth watered.

The pigs saw the wolf and they said, "Not by the hairs on our chinny-chin-chins."

The very hungry wolf was very mad. He shouted, "Then I'll huff and I'll puff and I'll blow your house in!" And the wolf huffed and he puffed and he blew the house in. The two little pigs ran to the third pig's brick house.

The mad, hungry, tired wolf followed the pigs. He saw the house of bricks. He walked up to the door. *Tap, tap, tap.* "Little Pigs, Little Pigs, let me come in." The wolf's mouth watered and his stomach growled.

The pigs saw the wolf and they said, "Not by the hairs on our chinny-chin-chins."

The very, very hungry wolf was very, very mad. He shouted, "Then I'll huff and I'll puff and I'll blow your house in!" And the wolf huffed and he puffed. And he huffed and he puffed. And he huffed and he puffed.

The little brick house stood strong. The three little pigs were safe inside. And the wolf? He was so hungry, so mad, and so tired. He ran into the woods and he never came back. The three little pigs lived safely in the little brick house for many years.

Name _____

Questions about
The Three Little Pigs

1. What three things did the pigs use to build their houses?

_____

_____

_____

2. Why did the wolf visit the little pigs?

_____

3. Why did the third house stand strong?

_____

_____

Paste the words in the correct boxes.

| paste | paste | paste | paste |
| paste | paste | paste | paste |

- ✂ - - - -

| on our | Little Pigs, | let me | Not by |
| Little Pigs, | the hairs | chinny-chin-chins. | come in. |

     Fairy Tales & Folktales • EMC 756

Name _____

What Does It Mean?

The wolf's mouth watered.
○ The wolf was tired.   ○ The wolf was hungry.   ○ The wolf was happy.

The wolf's stomach growled.
○ The wolf was thirsty.   ○ The wolf was lost.   ○ The wolf was hungry.

The brick house stood strong.
○ The wolf couldn't blow the house down.   ○ The wolf blew the house down.

Make a list of three things that **make your mouth water**.

1. _____

2. _____

3. _____

Make a list of three times that your **stomach has growled**.

1. _____

2. _____

3. _____

Make a list of three things that would **stand strong in a big windstorm**.

1. _____

2. _____

3. _____

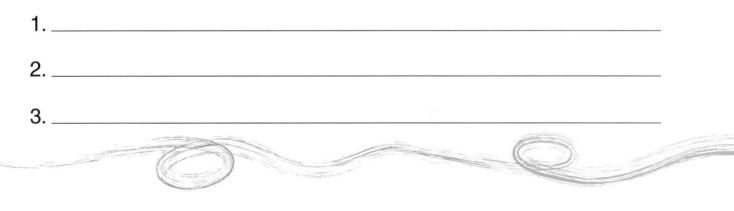

Name _____

Real or Make-Believe?

Mark Yes or No.

A wolf can blow down a house.

Yes   No

A pig can build a house of bricks.

Yes   No

A wolf can catch his dinner.

Yes   No

A pig can take a mud bath.

Yes   No

Little Red Riding Hood

In a little house by the woods there lived a happy little girl. She loved to pick flowers and listen to the birds sing. She wore a red cape with a little red hood. So she was called Little Red Riding Hood.

Little Red Riding Hood's mother asked her to take a basket of cookies to her grandmother. Grandmother lived on the other side of the woods. Little Red Riding Hood took the basket. Her mother said, "Don't stop along the way. Don't talk to strangers. There are dangers in the woods."

Little Red Riding Hood took the basket and skipped off along the path. She picked some flowers and put them in the basket. Then she stopped to listen to the birds sing. Little Red Riding Hood started off down the path again. A big wolf stepped out from behind a tree. "Where are you going, little girl?"

Red Riding Hood smiled. She said, "I'm taking these to my grandmother. She lives on the other side of the woods. But I mustn't stop. My mother says that there are dangers in the woods."

The wolf smiled, "Your mother is right. Hurry on to your grandmother's house." Soon Little Red Riding Hood was out of sight. The wolf ran ahead to Grandmother's house. He knocked on the door.

A voice from inside asked, "Who is there?"

"It is I, Little Red Riding Hood. I have brought you a basket of cookies," said the wolf. Grandmother opened the door. The wolf grabbed her and locked her in the closet. He put on Grandmother's nightgown. He climbed into her bed.

Just a few minutes later, Little Red Riding Hood knocked on Grandmother's door. "Grandmother, Grandmother, I have cookies and flowers for you."

From inside a voice called out, "Come in. Come in. I'm in my bed."

Little Red Riding Hood hurried into Grandmother's bedroom. She saw the wolf's big eyes. She said, "Oh, Grandmother, what big eyes you have!"

The wolf answered in a sweet grandmotherly voice, "All the better to see you, my dear."

Then Little Red Riding Hood saw the wolf's big ears. She said, "Oh, Grandmother, what big ears you have!"

The wolf answered meekly, "All the better to hear you, my dear."

Then Little Red Riding Hood saw the wolf's big white teeth. She said, "Oh, Grandmother, what big teeth you have."

The wolf jumped out of bed and grabbed Little Red Riding Hood. "All the better to eat you, my dear."

Little Red Riding Hood screamed. A hunter in the woods heard the scream. He rushed to Grandmother's house. He caught the wolf and saved Little Red Riding Hood. Together they found Grandmother in the closet. Grandmother and Little Red Riding Hood asked the hunter to share the cookies. When Little Red Riding Hood went home, the hunter walked with her through the woods.

Fairy Tales & Folktales • EMC 756

Name _____

Questions about
Little Red Riding Hood

1. What two things did Little Red Riding Hood's mother tell her not to do?

_____

_____

2. Why did Little Red Riding Hood stop in the woods?

_____

_____

3. What did the wolf tell Little Red Riding Hood to do?

_____

4. What three things about Grandmother seemed strange to Little Red Riding Hood?

_____

_____

_____

5. Who was the hero in this story? Tell why.

_____

_____

_____

_____

What Happened Next?

Cut out the sentences.
Paste them in order.
Circle the words to show who was talking.

1.

paste

Mother   **Little Red Riding Hood**   **Big Bad Wolf**

2.

paste

Mother   **Little Red Riding Hood**   **Big Bad Wolf**

3.

paste

Mother   **Little Red Riding Hood**   **Big Bad Wolf**

4.

paste

Mother   **Little Red Riding Hood**   **Big Bad Wolf**

5.

paste

Mother   **Little Red Riding Hood**   **Big Bad Wolf**

All the better to eat you, my dear.

Grandmother, what big teeth you have!

Where are you going, little girl?

I'm taking these to my grandmother.

Don't talk to strangers.

Name _____

When It Belongs to Someone

We use **'s** to show that something belongs to someone.
The house belonged to Grandmother so we say it was
Grandmother**'s** house.

Circle the words with **'s**. Finish the sentences to tell what belongs
to someone.

1. Little Red Riding Hood's cape was red.

   The cape belonged to _____.

2. Mother's basket was filled with cookies.

   The basket belonged to _____.

3. The wolf put on Grandmother's nightgown.

   The nightgown belonged to _____.

4. Little Red Riding Hood knocked on Grandmother's door.

   The door belonged to _____.

5. Little Red Riding Hood saw the wolf's big eyes.

   The eyes belonged to _____.

6. The hunter ate some of Grandmother's cookies.

   The cookies belonged to _____.

Goldilocks and the Three Bears

Once upon a time there were three bears—Mama Bear, Papa Bear, and Baby Bear. The bears lived in a cozy house by the edge of the woods. Every morning Mama Bear put their porridge in bowls to cool. Then the bears went for a walk before breakfast.

One morning a little girl came to the house by the edge of the woods. The little girl had yellow curls. Everyone called her Goldilocks. Goldilocks was curious. She wondered who lived in the cozy little house. She tapped on the door. When no one came, Goldilocks walked inside.

She saw three bowls of porridge on the table. Goldilocks was hungry. She picked up a spoon and ate a bite from the biggest bowl. It was too hot. She ate a bite from the middle-size bowl. It was too cold. Then she ate a bite from the baby bowl. It was just right, so Goldilocks ate it all up.

Goldilocks saw three chairs by the window. She sat in the biggest chair. It was too hard. She sat in the middle-size chair. It was too soft. Then she sat in the baby chair. It was just right.

Goldilocks was tired. She wanted to rest. She walked into the bears' bedroom. Goldilocks saw a big bed. She climbed onto the bed to rest. It was too bumpy. Goldilocks saw a middle-size bed. She climbed onto the bed to rest. It was too smooth. Goldilocks saw a baby bed. She climbed onto the bed to rest. It was just right, so Goldilocks fell asleep.

Soon the three bears returned home. Something was wrong.

Papa said, "Someone has been eating my porridge."

Mama said, "Someone has been eating my porridge."

Baby said, "Someone has been eating my porridge and it's all gone!"

The Bear family looked around.

Papa said, "Someone has been sitting in my chair."

Mama said, "Someone has been sitting in my chair."

Baby said, "Someone has been sitting in my chair and it's broken!"

The Bear family looked around again.

Papa said, "Someone has been on my bed."

Mama said, "Someone has been on my bed."

Baby said, "Someone has been on my bed and she's still here!"

Goldilocks woke up and saw the three bears. She jumped off the bed and ran out of the house. She didn't stop until she was home.

The three bears cleaned up their house and put a new lock on the door. Goldilocks never visited their house again.

Name _____

Questions about
Goldilocks and the Three Bears

1. Who were the characters in this story?

_____

_____

2. Draw the three different things that Goldilocks found in the bears' house.

3. What was always the same about the things Goldilocks liked?

_____

4. Why did the bears put a new lock on the door?

_____

_____

5. Why didn't Goldilocks visit the bears again?

_____

_____

Color Rhymes

Color the bowls. Draw two things in each bowl that rhyme with its color.

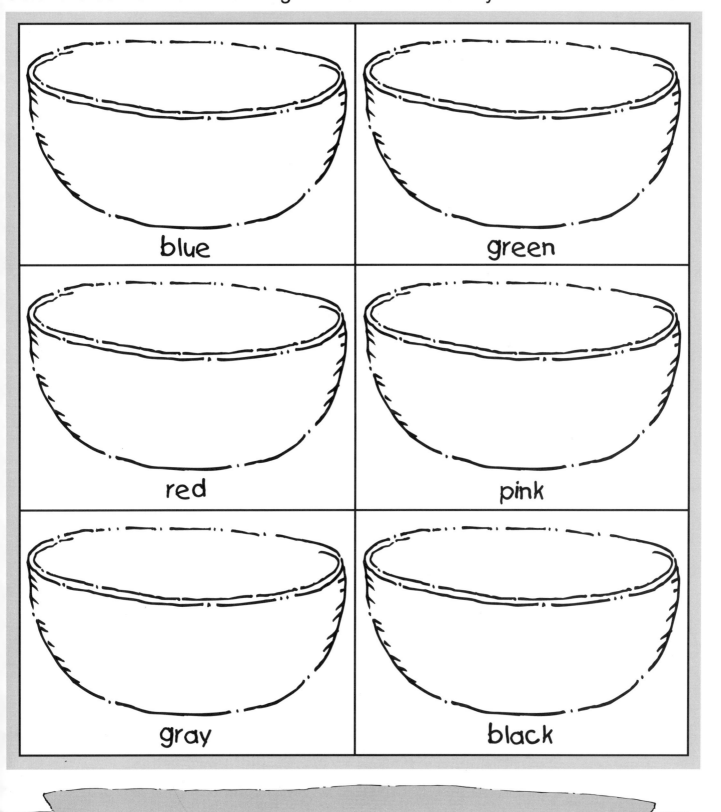

blue

green

red

pink

gray

black

Fairy Tales & Folktales • EMC 756

Name _____

Soft and Hard

Think of things that are soft and things that are hard.
Draw them in the correct place. Write a word to tell what each thing is.

Is anything soft and hard at the same time? Put it in the middle section labeled **Both**.

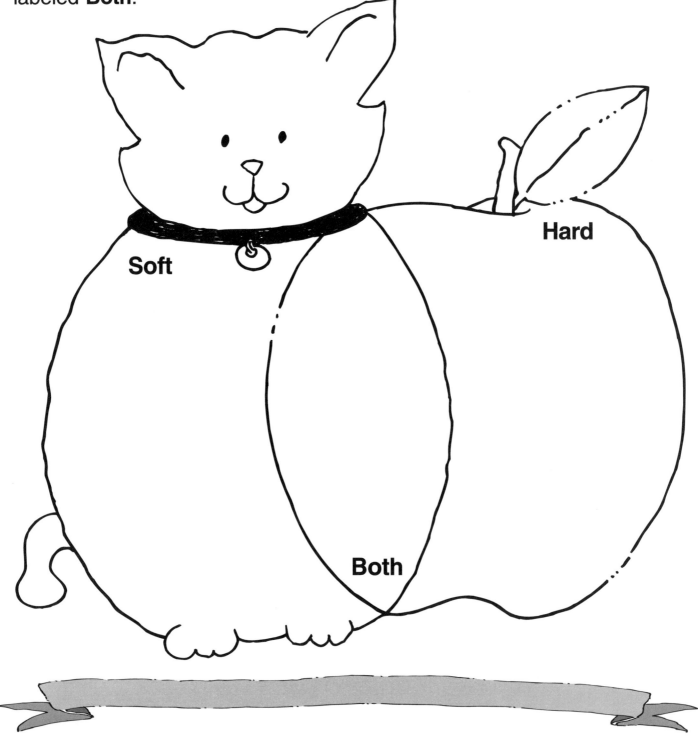

Soft

Hard

Both

Jack and the Beanstalk

Jack and his mother were hungry. There was no food in the house. Jack's mother told Jack to sell the cow. "Be quick, Jack."

So Jack led the cow away. On his way he met an old man. "You there, stop. Sell me your cow. I will give you these magic beans for her."

Jack remembered his mother's words, "Be quick!" He gave the old man the cow and took the magic beans. He hurried home.

Jack's mother looked up as Jack opened the door. "Home so soon? Good boy, Jack. How much did you get for the cow?" Jack held out his hand. He showed his mother the magic beans. "Only a handful of beans? How will we buy food? What will we eat?" she asked.

Jack looked at the beans in his hand. "But Mother, the beans are magic."

"Magic? Jack, there is no such thing as a magic bean." Jack's mother took the beans from Jack. She threw them into the garden. Then Jack and his mother went to bed. Their stomachs were as empty as their cupboard.

In the morning, Jack's growling stomach woke him early. He looked outside. He saw a giant beanstalk in the garden. Jack ran to the beanstalk. He began climbing. Jack climbed and climbed.

At the top he found himself in a new place. Everything was very big. The growling in Jack's stomach reminded him to look for food. Jack saw a giant house just ahead. He crawled up the steps. He knocked on the door. A woman opened it. "What can I do for you, little man?"

"Please, ma'am, my mother and I are hungry. Could you give me some food?" begged Jack.

"Little man, how did you get here to the giant's house?"

"I climbed a beanstalk that grew from magic beans."

The woman looked at Jack. "The giant will eat you if he finds you here. But since you are polite I will help you. Take this cheese and hurry home."

Jack ran to the beanstalk with the cheese on his back. As he neared the stalk, the ground shook. He heard the giant running after him. "Fee, fi, fo, fum. I know an Englishman has come!"

Jack jumped onto the beanstalk. He slid down as the giant roared in anger. Jack gave the cheese to his mother. They ate until their stomachs were full.

Fairy Tales & Folktales • EMC 756

The next morning, Jack climbed the beanstalk again. He knocked on the giant's door. The woman opened the door. She looked down on Jack. "You are a brave little man. Why have you come back? The giant is very angry."

"I came to thank you, ma'am. You have been kind."

"Little man, you must go. Take this bit of meat." The woman handed Jack a bag. With a smile and a nod, Jack turned to go. The bag was big. Jack ran as fast as he could. The beanstalk was just ahead when Jack heard the giant. "Fee, fi, fo, fum. I smell the smell of an Englishman!" The giant reached for Jack like a hungry monkey might reach for a banana. Jack dove for the top of the beanstalk. He scrambled down. The giant followed. The stalk shook with each giant step.

Jack called to his mother below to get the ax. He fell to the ground and began chopping the stalk. Just as the giant's foot came into view, the beanstalk toppled. The giant smashed to the ground. Jack's magic beanstalk was gone. The coins in the dead giant's pockets fed Jack and his mother for many days to come.

Name _____

Questions about
Jack and the Beanstalk

Cut and paste to put the story in order.

1.

| paste |

2.

| paste |

3.

| paste |

4.

| paste |

5.

| paste |

6.

| paste |

7.

| paste |

8.

| paste |

9.

| paste |

10.

| paste |

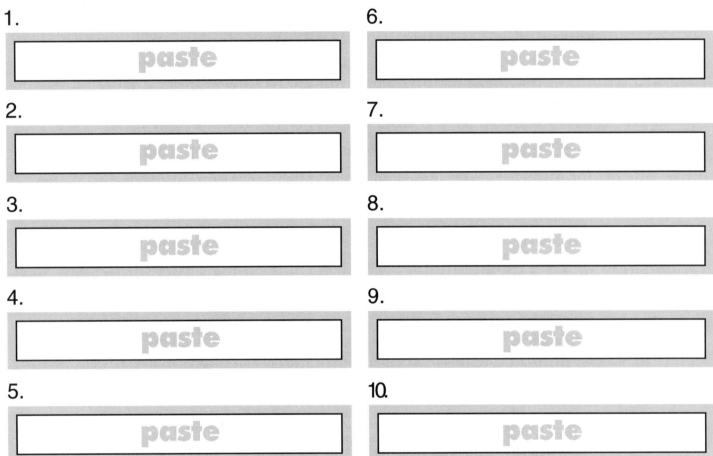

Jack and his mother bought food.	Jack climbed the beanstalk.
The giant chased Jack.	Jack and his mother ate cheese.
Jack sold the cow.	Jack's mother was angry.
Jack climbed the beanstalk.	The beanstalk grew.
Jack chopped down the beanstalk.	Jack knocked at the door.

Name _____

Learning about Characters

Mark Yes or No. Write a sentence to tell why you marked that answer.

Jack was helpful.	Yes	No
Jack was very shy.	Yes	No
Jack was brave.	Yes	No

The woman was kind.	Yes	No
The woman was selfish.	Yes	No

103 Fairy Tales & Folktales • EMC 756

Name _____

Making Comparisons

| Jack and his mother were hungry. Their stomachs were **as empty as their cupboard**. |

Finish the sentences to tell about your stomach.

When I am hungry, my stomach is as empty as _____.

When I am full, my stomach is as full as _____.

| The giant wanted to catch Jack. He reached for Jack **like a hungry monkey might reach for a banana**. |

Finish the sentences to tell about reaching for a special treat.

I wanted a special treat. I reached for the treat like _____.

What treat would you reach for? _____

● ● ● Special Meanings ● ● ●

The story says that Jack's growling stomach did two things. What were they?

1. _____

2. _____

The story says that the coins in the giant's pockets fed Jack and his mother. What does that mean?

_____

_____

An Ant's Voice

An East African Tale

Once upon a time an ant went to find a new house. He crawled into a lizard's home when the lizard was away. He made himself at home. When the lizard came back, it saw new tracks going into its cave. The lizard called, "Who's in my house?"

? Setting.

Problem

The ant yelled out in a loud voice, "It is I! I am so strong I trample elephants as I pass. Who dares to ask?" The tiny ant's voice boomed through the cave.

The lizard ran away from its home, crying, "What can I do? I cannot fight a creature who tramples elephants. How will I get my house back?"

Soon the lizard met a warthog. It asked the warthog for help. When they reached the mouth of the cave, the warthog barked loudly, "Who is in the house of my friend the lizard?"

The ant answered in a loud voice. "It is I! I am so strong I trample elephants as I pass. Who dares to ask?"

The warthog backed away from the cave. "I am sorry. I can do nothing," it said, and quickly left.

Then the lizard stopped a tiger that was passing by. The tiger told the lizard not to worry. The tiger moved to the mouth of the cave. It showed its claws and growled, "Who is in the house of my friend the lizard?"

The ant shouted back, "It is I! I am so powerful I trample elephants as I pass. Who dares to ask?"

The tiger jumped back. "The creature tramples elephants! What will it do to me? I cannot help you, friend."

The lizard was about to give up hope. Then it saw a little frog passing by. The lizard stopped the frog and asked for help. The frog went to the mouth of the cave. It asked who was inside. The ant gave the same answer, "It is I! I am so powerful I trample elephants as I pass. Who dares to ask?"

The frog took one hop into the cave and croaked back, "I, who have come at last, I dare to ask. I am the most powerful of all. I am the one who tramples those who trample elephants!"

When the ant heard this, he shook. He saw the big shadow at the mouth of the cave. He thought, "Look at the awful thing that has come to get me. I have had my fun. I have stayed in the cave long enough." The ant crept out of the cave.

The lizard and the other animals nearby pounced on the ant. "You!" the animals cried. "You are only an ant! The cave's echo made your voice big and loud. We thought you were big and mean."

The ant stared at the frog. "And you, Frog, your shadow made me think you were huge."

The animals laughed at themselves. The ant scurried away.

Name _____

Questions about
An Ant's Voice

1. What animal lived in the cave?

_____

2. What animal made itself at home in the cave?

_____

3. How did the animal answer the other animals' questions?

_____

_____

4. What animal was able to make the cave visitor leave?

_____

5. Why was the ant's voice so loud?

_____

_____

6. Why was the frog's shadow so big?

_____

_____

_____

Name _____

What Does It Mean?

Complete the sentences using the words in the Word Box.

1. A rhinoceros is a _____ animal.

2. An elephant _____ the grass when it runs.

3. The ant's voice _____ through the cave.

4. The little mouse _____ along.

5. The tiger _____ on its dinner.

Word Box		
tramples	scurried	echoed
pounced	powerful	

● ● ● Pronouns ● ● ●

Read each sentence. Tell what character or characters the underlined word is talking about.

1. The tiger moved to the mouth of the cave.
   <u>It</u> showed its claws.   _____

2. The warthog and the lizard walked to the cave.
   When <u>they</u> got there the warthog barked.   _____

3. The lizard and the other animals pounced on
   the ant. "<u>You!</u>" the animals cried.   _____

 Fairy Tales & Folktales • EMC 756

Name _____

The Sound of o

Different letters make the sound of long **o**.

ow—shad**ow**   **oa**—cr**oa**k   **o**—ech**o**   **o**-**e**—h**o**m**e**

Write the words above to complete the sentences. Then circle the letters that make the long **o** sound.

1. The frog's _____ scared the ant.

2. The frog's _____ was loud.

3. The voice in the cave made an _____.

4. The lizard wanted its _____.

Mark the pictures that have the long **o** sound.

Name _____

Opposites

Color in the circles to show the opposites.

big	○ little	○ huge	○ rig
weak	○ meek	○ beak	○ strong
loud	○ crowd	○ quiet	○ noisy
stop	○ halt	○ go	○ crop
ask	○ answer	○ question	○ task
laugh	○ half	○ giggle	○ cry

Now underline to show the words that have the **same** meaning.

What is alike about all the unmarked words?

_____

Draw two things that are opposites.

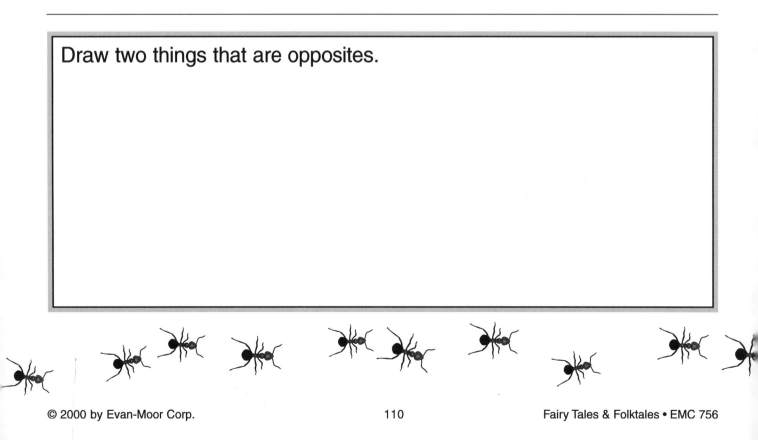

The Stars in the Sky

An English Tale

Once upon a time there was a little girl. She wanted to touch the stars in the sky. The little girl asked her father and her mother if they could get them for her. They told her not to be silly.

So the little girl set off on her own to find the stars. She came to an old windmill beside a pond. She asked the pond, "If you please, have you seen the stars in the sky?"

"Yes," said the pond. "The stars often come and play in my water. Jump in and swim. Perhaps you will find them."

So the little girl jumped into the pond. She swam and swam. She did not find the stars. She swam to a meadow where the fairies played. She asked the fairies, "Have you seen the stars in the sky? I would like to touch them."

"Yes," said the fairies. "We have seen the stars. They often shine in the grass at our feet. Dance with us. Perhaps you will find them."

So the little girl danced and danced. Still she couldn't find the stars. She was very tired. She sat down on the grass and cried. "I have swum. I have danced. But I have not found the stars."

"Little girl," the fairies said, "follow this path. Remember these words. Perhaps then you will find the stars." Together the fairies chanted, "Four-Feet must carry Two-Feet to No-Feet-At-All. Climb the stair with no steps to touch the stars so tall."

The little girl thanked the fairies for their help. She started down the path. She whispered the fairies' words over and over. Before long she came to a dark forest. A pony was tied to a tree at the edge of the forest.

"The fairies have sent me to you," the little girl said. "They told me, 'Four-Feet must carry Two-Feet to No-Feet-At-All. Climb the stair with no steps to touch the stars so tall.' "

"Climb on then," said the pony. "I will help you." The pony carried the little girl through the forest to the edge of the sea. The pony stopped there. It said, "Look straight ahead and you will see No-Feet-At-All."

The little girl peered into the dark water in front of her. A strange fish appeared. "Are you No-Feet-At-All?" the little girl asked. "Will you take me to the stair with no steps?"

"I will help you. Jump on my back!" said the fish. The little girl jumped onto the fish's back. The fish swam to an arc of many colors in the sky. I have brought you to the stair with no steps. Good-bye." The little girl climbed off. The fish flipped back into the dark sea.

The little girl stood alone at the bottom of the beautiful arc. It glowed above her head. She felt very small. Slowly she began to climb. She climbed and she climbed. The shining stars were above her. Then she looked down. She was so high that her head began to spin. She slipped and fell. Down, down, down she dropped.

She might have been falling still if she had not struck the floor in her own bedroom and found that it was morning.

Name _____

1. What did the little girl want to do?

_____

2. Why did the little girl set off on her own?

_____

3. What did the little girl do to find the stars?

_____

_____

4. Who was Four-Feet?

5. Who was Two-Feet?

6. Who was No-Feet-At-All?

7. Did the little girl touch the stars?

_____

8. Do you think the little girl really swam, danced, and rode?
   Explain your answer.

_____

_____

Name _____

What Happened Next?

Color, cut, and paste to put the sentences in order.
Then draw a picture to show each thing.

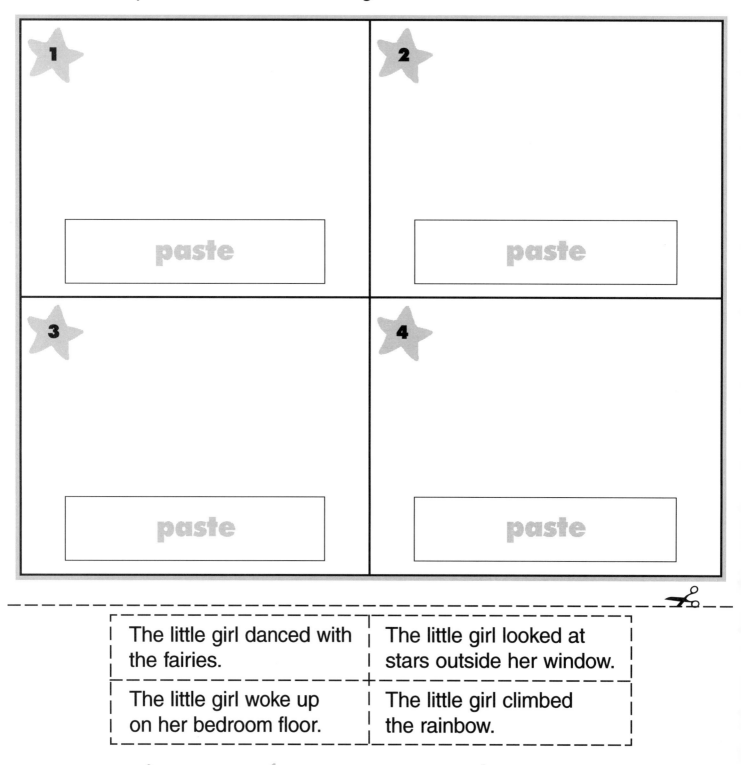

1	2
paste	paste
3	4
paste	paste

✂ -

The little girl danced with the fairies.	The little girl looked at stars outside her window.
The little girl woke up on her bedroom floor.	The little girl climbed the rainbow.

114   Fairy Tales & Folktales • EMC 756

Name _____

What Did I Say?

Match each character to what it said.

"Don't be silly!"

"Climb the stair with no steps to touch the stars so tall."

"If you please, have you seen the stars in the sky?"

"Jump in and swim."

"Climb on then. I will help you."

"I have brought you to the stair with no steps. Good-bye."

Name _____

Which Word Is Best?

Circle the words that complete the sentences.

1. I want to _____ in the pool.   swim   swam

   Sammy _____ all day yesterday.   swim   swam

2. Will you _____ with me?   dance   danced

   Cinderella and her prince _____ at the ball.   dance   danced

3. The fairies told the little girl to _____ the stair.   climb   climbed

   The little girl _____ so high she got dizzy.   climb   climbed

4. I _____ a letter to my grandma.   send   sent

   Will you _____ a postcard?   send   sent

116   Fairy Tales & Folktales • EMC 756

Two Goats on the Bridge

A Tale from Russia

Between two tall hills lay a narrow bridge. On each hill lived a goat. Some days the goat from the hill on the west would cross the bridge. It would eat the green grass on the hill on the east. Some days the goat from the hill on the east would cross the bridge. It would eat the green grass on the hill on the west. One day both goats began to cross the bridge at the same time.

The goats met in the middle of the bridge. Neither wanted to give way. "Move off!" shouted the goat from the west. "I am crossing this bridge."

"Move yourself!" snorted the goat from the east. "I am crossing here!"

Neither goat would go back. Neither goat could go forward. They stood nose-to-nose for a long time. Then they put down their heads and began to push. They were both strong. They pushed and shoved. And they pushed and shoved. They pushed each other off the bridge.

Wet and angry, they climbed from the river. They shook themselves off. They looked at each other with accusing eyes. They stomped off to their own hills. Each muttered under his breath, "He is so stubborn. Just see the trouble he caused."

Name _____

Questions about
Two Goats on the Bridge

1. What happened to start the story?

_____

_____

2. What happened to end the story?

_____

_____

Folktales like this one have been told over and over in many different ways. Change the animals and the setting. Tell it again.

_____

_____

_____

_____

_____

_____

_____

_____

Name _____

Clues in the Story

Cut and paste the clues that the storyteller used.

The goats are stubborn.

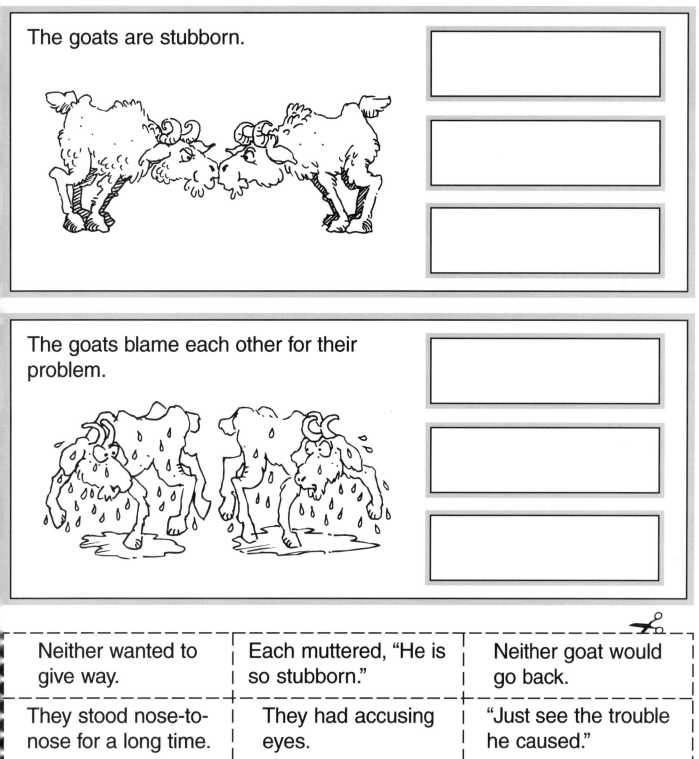

The goats blame each other for their problem.

Neither wanted to give way.	Each muttered, "He is so stubborn."	Neither goat would go back.
They stood nose-to-nose for a long time.	They had accusing eyes.	"Just see the trouble he caused."

Fairy Tales & Folktales • EMC 756

Name _____

Crossword Puzzle

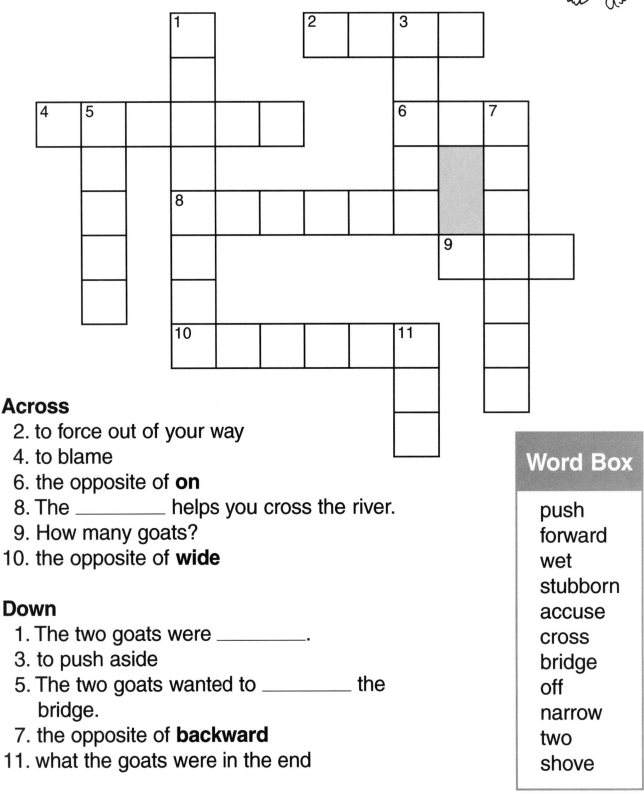

Across

2. to force out of your way
4. to blame
6. the opposite of **on**
8. The _____ helps you cross the river.
9. How many goats?
10. the opposite of **wide**

Down

1. The two goats were _____.
3. to push aside
5. The two goats wanted to _____ the bridge.
7. the opposite of **backward**
11. what the goats were in the end

Word Box

push
forward
wet
stubborn
accuse
cross
bridge
off
narrow
two
shove

Name _____

Working with Word Families

-een

qu + een = ___ ___ ___ ___ ___   s + een = ___ ___ ___ ___

gr + een = ___ ___ ___ ___ ___   t + een = ___ ___ ___ ___

k + een = ___ ___ ___ ___   scr + een = ___ ___ ___ ___ ___ ___

Use the new words to make compound words.

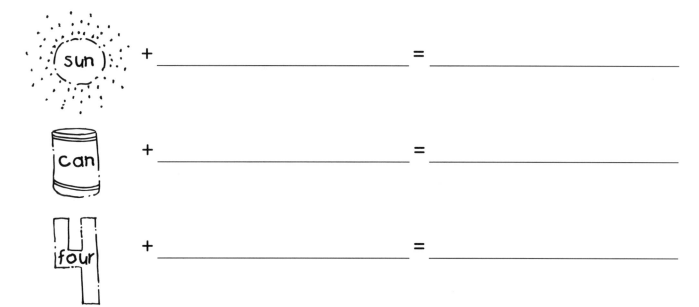

sun + _____ = _____

can + _____ = _____

four + _____ = _____

Write a sentence for each of the new compound words.

_____

_____

_____

Hansel and Gretel

Once there was a poor woodcutter. He was very poor. He had no food for his children, Hansel and Gretel. One night the children went to bed. Their stepmother said, "We do not have enough food. We will starve if we go on feeding your children! Let us leave them in the woods."

The little boy heard his father and his stepmother. He made a plan. He filled his pockets with small white pebbles.

The next morning the stepmother woke the children, "Come with us to cut wood." She gave them each a crust of bread. They went into the woods. Hansel dropped his pebbles along the path. When they were deep in the woods, their father built a fire. He told the boy and girl to wait until he returned. The children fell asleep.

 Fairy Tales & Folktales • EMC 756

When they woke up, the fire was out. It was dark. "Father forgot us!" cried Gretel. Hansel showed her his trail of pebbles. The pebbles were shining in the moonlight. They followed them home. Their father was happy to see them.

The stepmother was mad. She took the children into the woods again. This time Hansel had no pebbles. He dropped crumbs of his bread along the path. Again the children fell asleep. When they woke up, Hansel looked for the trail of crumbs. The birds had eaten every crumb.

The children wandered through the woods. They were hungry and scared. They came to a clearing. In the clearing was a candy house. The children broke pieces off the house and ate them.

Suddenly a voice said, "Nibble, nibble like a mouse. Who is nibbling on my house?" They looked up to see an old witch with thick glasses. The witch peered at the boy and girl. Then she grabbed Hansel. She threw him into a cage. She said to Gretel, "Come, little girl, you must cook. When your brother is plump, I will eat him."

Each day the witch went to the bars of Hansel's cage. She told him to stick out a finger. Hansel wanted to trick the witch. He stuck a stick through the bars. The witch would peer at the stick. Then she would mutter, "Still too thin!" and stomp away.

 Fairy Tales & Folktales • EMC 756

One day the witch decided to eat Hansel, thin or fat. She built a fire in the oven. She told Gretel to see if it was hot. Gretel was afraid for Hansel. She wanted to trick the witch. She whined, "I don't know how to do it. Will you show me?"

"Silly girl!" screamed the witch. "I'll do it myself." She opened the oven door and peered inside.

In a flash, Gretel pushed the witch into the oven. She slammed the door closed and ran to Hansel. The children ran and ran through the woods. They found themselves back at their own house. Their happy father told them that their stepmother was gone. The children hugged him. From that day on they took care of each other, even in hard times.

 Fairy Tales & Folktales • EMC 756

Name _____

Questions about
Hansel and Gretel

Match to tell about the characters.

Hansel   wanted to leave the children in the woods.

Gretel   wanted to eat a plump child.

Father   left a trail of white pebbles.

Stepmother   trapped the witch in the oven.

Witch   was happy to see Hansel and Gretel.

● ● ● ● ● ● ● ● ● ● ● ● ● ● ● ● ● ●

The story ends saying, "From that day on they took care of each other, even in hard times." Tell what you think that means.

_____

_____

_____

_____

_____

_____

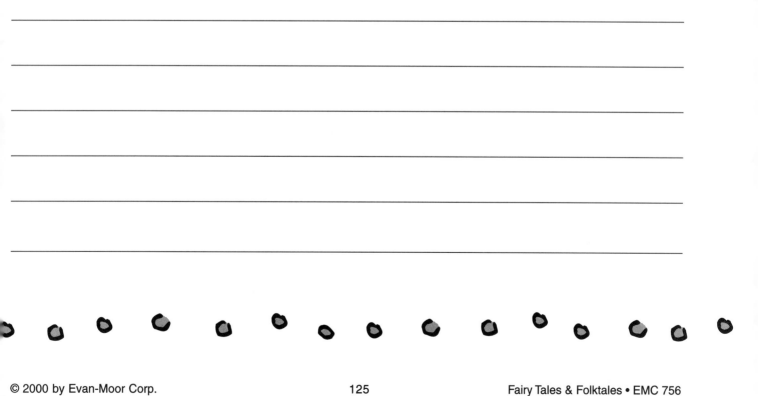

Name _____

The Sound of *ar*

Listen to the sound of **ar** in these words.

b**ar**   st**ar**ve   h**ar**d

Now make new **-ar** words.

y ___ ___ d   c ___ ___ d   f ___ ___

j ___ ___   st ___ ___   c ___ ___ ve

Use the new words to complete these sentences.

1. My cousin lives _____ away.

2. I like to play in my _____.

3. I will send you a birthday _____.

4. Are there any pickles in the _____?

5. Dad will _____ the turkey.

6. Mrs. Smith put a _____ on my paper.

Write a sentence of your own. Use an **-ar** word.

_____

_____

Name _____

Sort by Syllables

Say each word in the Word Box. Count how many syllables it has.
Then write the word in the correct list.

Word Box				
woodcutter	starve	stepmother	plump	shining
poor	outside	built	pocket	asleep
enough	candy	grabbed	finger	children

One-Syllable Words	Two-Syllable Words	Three-Syllable Words

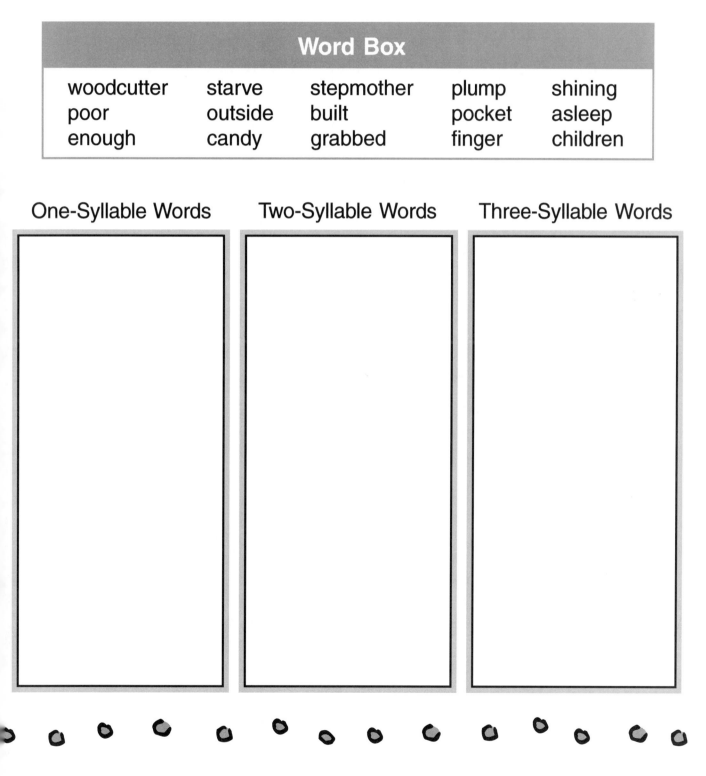

The Hungry Troll

A Tale from Denmark

Once there was a poor man. He sat down under a tree. He began to eat his bit of bread. A tiny dwarf walked up. The dwarf had a bent back and a long white beard. "Could you spare a coin for this old man?"

The poor man looked up. "I have no spare coins," he said. "But will you share my bread?"

The dwarf was hungry. So he ate half of the bread. He nodded to the poor man. He twirled around three times and vanished.

The poor man stood up to go. He heard loud steps—stomp! stomp! stomp! The steps were coming toward him. He looked up to see a big, ugly troll.

Fairy Tales & Folktales • EMC 756

"You are in my woods!" the troll shouted.

"I'm just passing through," said the poor man. "I will soon be gone."

"I am hungry. So I will eat you. Then you will be gone!"

"Please don't!" cried the man. "I have a wife and six children. Think of how sad they will be if you kill me."

"You make a good point," said the troll. "I will give you a chance. We will play a game. You hide. I will find you. If I can find you three times, I will cook you in my pot."

The troll turned and walked away. The poor man looked around. He saw the old dwarf standing behind him. "Don't worry. I'll help you hide," said the dwarf.

The dwarf chopped a piece of bark from a tree. He pushed the poor man inside the tree. He put the bark back.

Soon the troll came. He had a big ax on his shoulder. He muttered, "I'll chop down a tree. I'll chop down a tree." He walked up to the poor man's tree. He cut it down with one blow. He pulled the poor man out. "You lose once!" he laughed. And off he went.

The dwarf came back. "We will not let him win. Come with me." He took the poor man to a lake. There were reeds growing at the edge of the lake. He tapped the poor man with his cane. The man became the size of an ant. The dwarf put the man inside a reed. He stuck the reed in the mud.

Before long the troll came back. This time he brought a big knife. He muttered, "I'll cut the reeds. I'll cut the reeds." He whacked the reeds with his knife. Then he shook them. The poor man fell out. He returned to his normal size. "That's twice you lose!" the troll laughed. And off he went.

The poor man started to cry. The dwarf appeared again. "Cheer up! We have one more chance." He clapped his hands. The poor man turned into a fish. The dwarf tossed the fish into the lake.

The troll walked up carrying a tub and a fishing pole. He muttered, "I'll catch a fish. I'll catch a fish." He put the tub in the water. He climbed in it. He pushed off and cast his line. The dwarf stood by the lake. He blew out three big breaths. The wind howled. A storm stirred the water. The troll screamed from his tub. The tub tipped over. The troll fell out and sank to the bottom of the lake.

The wind stopped. The dwarf clapped his hands three times. The poor man was himself again. "Thank you for sharing your bread, sir," said the dwarf. And he was gone.

The poor man went home to his family. He never saw the dwarf again.

Name _____

Questions about
The Hungry Troll

Choose the best answer.

1. What did the dwarf want?
   ○ a coin   ○ some food   ○ a friend

2. What did the poor man give the dwarf?
   ○ a coin   ○ some bread   ○ a ride

3. Who didn't want the poor man in the woods?
   ○ the dwarf   ○ the troll   ○ his wife and six children

4. How many chances did the poor man have to win in the troll's game?
   ○ 1   ○ 2   ○ 3

5. Why did the dwarf help the poor man?
   ○ He didn't like the troll.   ○ The poor man had helped him.

6. What happened to the troll?
   ○ He sank to the bottom of the lake.   ○ He went home to his family.

7. Which character is the "bad guy" in the story?
   ○ the poor man   ○ the troll   ○ the dwarf

8. Who was hungry?
   ○ the dwarf   ○ the troll   ○ both the troll and the dwarf

Name _____

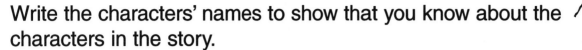

Looking at the Characters

Write the characters' names to show that you know about the characters in the story.

_____ had a bent back.

_____ was big and ugly.

_____ didn't have a spare coin.

_____ helped the man hide.

_____ carried an ax.

_____ had a wife and six children.

_____ had a white beard.

_____ cried because he was afraid.

_____ liked to play games.

Which character was your favorite? Tell why.

_____

_____

_____

132   Fairy Tales & Folktales • EMC 756

Working with Word Families

-are

b + are = ___ ___ ___ ___	sp + are = ___ ___ ___ ___ ___
Draw a bare foot.	Draw where you keep your spare tire.
sh + are = ___ ___ ___ ___ ___	squ + are = ___ ___ ___ ___ ___ ___
Draw something you would share.	Draw a square. Color it blue.
h + are = ___ ___ ___ ___	sc + are = ___ ___ ___ ___ ___
Who won the race—Tortoise or Hare? Draw the finish.	Draw something that would scare you.

Fairy Tales & Folktales • EMC 756

Slops

A Tale from Wales

There was once an old man and an old woman. They lived in a house with a wall all around it. Every night the old woman would peel potatoes and toss the peelings into the slop pail. Then she would peel carrots and toss the peelings into the slop pail. Then she would peel onions and toss the peelings into the slop pail. Later she would wash the dishes and pour the dirty water into the slop pail.

Then the old man would pick up the heavy pail. He would carry it outside. One, two, three, four, five, six, seven, eight, nine, ten steps to the front wall. He threw the slops over the wall. SLOSH!

One night the old man carried the slop pail outside. One, two, three, four, five, six, seven, eight, nine, ten steps...SLOSH! Then he heard a shrill voice. "Do you have to pour your slops down my chimney?"

The old man looked over the wall. He didn't see anything. He shook his head and walked back into his house.

The next night the old woman peeled potatoes and tossed the peelings into the slop pail. She peeled carrots and

Fairy Tales & Folktales • EMC 756

tossed the peelings into the slop pail. She peeled onions and tossed the peelings into the slop pail. Later she washed the dishes. She poured the dirty water into the slop pail.

Then the old man picked up the heavy pail. He carried it across the floor and out the door. One, two, three, four, five, six, seven, eight, nine, ten steps. He threw the slops over the front wall. SLOSH!

"Oh, no! You're doing it again. I wish you'd stop doing that! You are pouring slops right down my chimney! Do you hear what I am saying?"

"Yes, I hear what you are saying," said the old man. "But I don't know who you are and I don't see your house."

"Look here!" yelled the little man.

The old man peered over the wall. There was a little house! What a mess! There were potato peelings on the roof. Carrot peelings hung from the window. The yard was piled with onion skins. Dirty water ran down the roof.

"Oh, dear, I have been pouring my slops down your chimney!" said the old man.

The old man went back into his house and told his wife. "We must stop pouring our slops on the little house. But I cannot carry the pail around the house. It is too heavy."

The old woman had an idea. "What if we had a door in back?" she asked. "You could carry the pail ten steps out the back door. Then you could throw the slops over the back wall."

"What a good idea!" said the old man. "The town carpenter can make us a new back door."

Now the old woman fixes supper. She fills the slop pail. The old man carries the slop pail out the back door. One, two, three, four, five, six, seven, eight, nine, ten steps. He throws it over the back wall. SLOSH!

Every night the old man pushes open the new back door. Every night a tiny silver coin rolls out from under the door. It is left there—a gift—from one good neighbor to another.

 Fairy Tales & Folktales • EMC 756

Name _____

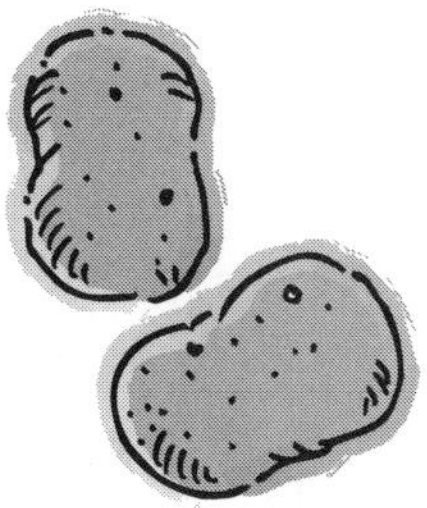

Questions about
Slops

1. How did this story get its name?

_____

_____

2. What four things did the old woman do every night?

_____

_____

_____

_____

3. How did the old man get rid of the slops?

_____

_____

4. What problem did this cause?

_____

_____

5. How did the old man and the old woman become good neighbors?

_____

_____

137   Fairy Tales & Folktales • EMC 756

Name _____

Where Did It Happen?

Reread the story and list some of the things you know about where it happened.

_____

_____

Use your list to draw the place.

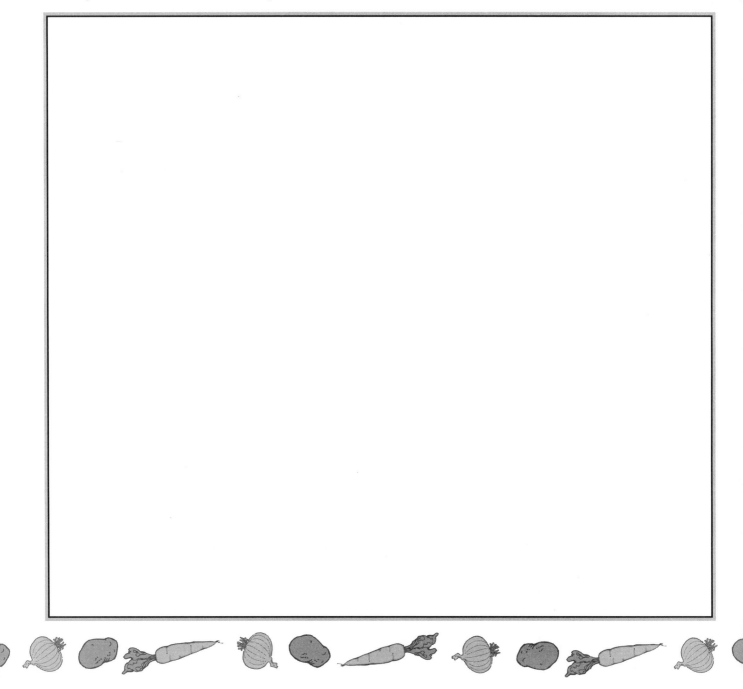

Name _____

Working with Word Families

-ail

Draw a picture to show what each word means.
Then write a sentence using the word.

sn + ail = ___ ___ ___ ___ ___

p + ail = ___ ___ ___ ___

_____

_____

_____

_____

m + ail = ___ ___ ___ ___

tr + ail = ___ ___ ___ ___ ___

_____

_____

_____

_____

Write some other **-ail** words here.

_____

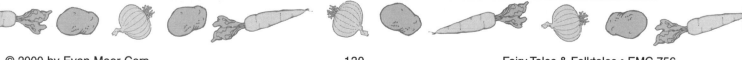

Fairy Tales & Folktales • EMC 756

Page 6
1. do her work
2. Grandpa
3. No problem!
4. louder
5. quieter
6. the same

Page 7

Page 8
Examples:
Loud—carpenter, fireman, drummer, workman
Quiet—keyboarder, librarian, someone sewing, doctor

Page 9
Colored pictures should include question mark, queen, quail, quarterback, quart of milk, quarter, and quilt.

Page 12
The kitten should be drawn.
The kitten and goat should be drawn.
The kitten, goat, and bear should be drawn.
The house exploded and everyone was blown up into the sky.

Page 13
Drawings will vary.

Page 14

Page 15
room, broom, bloom, groom

Drawings will vary.

Page 18
tusk—spear
side—wall
leg—tree trunk
ear—fan
tail—rope
trunk—snake

Each blind man touched only one part of the elephant.

Page 19

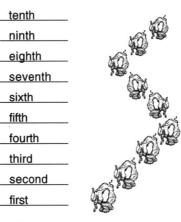

tenth
ninth
eighth
seventh
sixth
fifth
fourth
third
second
first

Page 20
find   wind
kind   blind
mind   grind

1. find
2. Wind
3. blind
4. kind
5. Mind
6. Grind

Page 21
feather—beginning, taffy—middle, giraffe—end, muffin—middle, fork—beginning, leaf—end

elephant, photo, graph

Page 24
1. The teeny-tiny woman lived in a teeny-tiny house.
2. The teeny-tiny woman buttoned her teeny-tiny coat, put on her teeny-tiny hat, and opened her teeny-tiny door.
3. She found a teeny-tiny bone.
4. The teeny-tiny woman took the bone home as a treat for her teeny-tiny dog.
5. No, the teeny-tiny woman told the voice to take it before she gave it to her dog.

Page 25

Page 26
louder, taller, softer
Pictures will vary. The second picture in each set should be comparatively more.

Page 27
Teeny-tiny Things—button, ant, tack, sprout
Great Big Things—mountain, ocean liner, hippo, truck

Page 31
1. her pig
2. Her pig wouldn't move.
3. a puddle
4. It was hot.

The boy began to swat the horsefly.
The horsefly began to sting the horse.
The horse began to drink the water.
The water began to put out the fire.
The fire began to burn the stick.
The stick began to beat the dog.
The dog began to bite the pig.
The pig jumped out of the puddle and ran home.

Page 32
The horse flicked his tail.
The pig sat in the puddle.
The fire burned.
The horsefly buzzed.

Drawings will vary.

Page 33
huddle, muddle, puddle, cuddle

1. puddle
2. huddle
3. cuddle
4. muddle

Drawings will vary.

Page 35
1. Two boys had an argument.
2. The boys' mother showed them how to set up three special sticks that would decide the winner.
3. No one was the winner.
4. By the time the sticks had fallen over, the boys had forgotten what the argument was about.
5. Answers will vary.

Page 36
argument—a fight
explain—to tell about
alone—by oneself
heap—a pile

1. argument
2. heap
3. alone
4. explain

Drawings will vary.

Page 37
Drawings will vary.

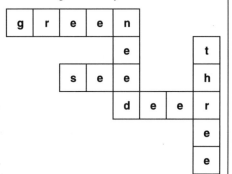

Page 38
toy, joy, boy, coin, join, noise, point, spoil

He wants a gum ball. See him point.

He puts a coin in the slot.

Wow! He gets a toy.

Page 41
1. The characters are a pumpkin named Feegba and a farmer.
2. The farmer tried to harvest the pumpkin. He started to cut it open.
3. The pumpkin was angry.
4. It started to roll toward the man, but when it hit a jagged rock it split open.
5. the shining stars
6. He was afraid that the pumpkin might start chasing him.

Page 42
knee, knot, knife, doorknob, knapsack, knight

Sentences will vary.

Page 43
Colored pictures should include key, jeep, needle, bee, seal, wheel, three, tree, ski, and pea.

Page 44
Drawings should show the comparisons.

Sentences will vary.

Page 47
1. Chicken Licken thought the sky was falling.
2. They all asked how Chicken Licken knew that the sky was falling.
3. Chicken Licken always answered, "A piece fell on my head."
4. No. Foxy Loxy was licking his chops when he told the others to come to his den. He wasn't afraid that the sky was falling; he was hungry!

Page 48
Rhymes may vary: Tiger Liger, Kitten Litten, Puppy Luppy, Hamster Lamster, Monkey Lonkey, Bunny Lunny

Henny Penny has a different rhyme because her last name starts with a P not an L.

Page 49
Chicken Licken walked down the road.
We are going to tell the king.
Help! The sky is falling!
Wait! Come to my den.

Page 50
1. sly
2. fly
3. cry
4. why
5. dry
6. fry

Page 53
3
5
4
1
9
7
2
6
8

Answers will vary.

Page 54
cook, book, hook, brook

Drawings will vary.

fishhook, notebook

Page 55

Page 56
Drawings will vary.

Page 60
1. The people of Hamlin wanted to get rid of their rats.
2. They offered a reward to anyone who could get rid of the rats.
3. The stranger was dressed in bright colors, with a wooden pipe in his belt. He seemed to dance when he walked.
4. He piped a tune and all the rats followed him. He led them to the river and they jumped in and drowned.
5. The mayor thought the piper hadn't worked hard enough to earn the reward.
6. The townsfolk "paid" the piper with their children because they wouldn't give him the reward.

Page 61
mouth, town, down, house, out, now, sound, drown

1. town
2. mouth
3. house
4. Now
5. drown
6. sound

Page 62

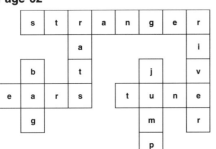

Page 66

1. yes
2. no
3. yes
4. yes
5. no
6. no
7. yes
8. yes
9. no

Page 67

filled, filling
worked, working
knocked, knocking
opened, opening
sewed, sewing

napped, napping
stopped, stopping
slammed, slamming

1. worked
2. napped
3. knocked
4. opened
5. filled

Page 68

yes, no
yes – Drawings will vary.

Page 71

1. patient
2. before the big egg
3. it was different
4. it was a graceful swan
5. a beautiful swan
6. Mother Duck was a good mother. She took care of the eggs and tried to protect the big gray duckling.

Page 72

Page 73

catch, latch
hatch, match
batch, patch

Drawings will vary.

Page 74

Students may state the moral/lesson in different ways. Some possible morals/lessons are: Looks can change. Just because something or someone is different, doesn't make it or the person ugly. You can't tell how someone will turn out.

Page 78

1. Rose didn't know how to carry things. When her father told her how to carry one thing, she tried to carry another thing that same way.
2. Her father always said, "What a fool!"
3. Rose always said, "OK, I'll do that next time."
4. Rose's father was the biggest fool. He didn't take the time to teach Rose how to carry things, and he didn't see that Rose worked hard.

Page 79

Drawings and sentences will vary.

Page 80

beach   teach
peach   reach
bleach   preach

My mother used <u>bleach</u> to get my shirt white.
I love <u>peach</u> ice cream.
I cannot <u>reach</u> the book.
Let's go to the <u>beach</u>.

Drawings will vary.

Page 84

1. The three little pigs used straw, sticks, and bricks.
2. The wolf was hungry and wanted to eat the pigs.
3. Bricks make stronger houses than sticks or straw.
Pigs—Not by the hairs on our chinny-chin-chins.
Wolf—Little Pigs, Little Pigs, let me come in.

Page 85

The wolf was hungry.
The wolf was hungry.
The wolf couldn't blow the house down.

Students' responses will vary.

Page 86

no, no,
yes, yes

Page 90

1. Her mother told her not to stop along the way and not to talk to strangers.
2. She stopped to listen to the birds sing and to pick flowers.
3. The wolf told her to hurry to her grandmother's house.
4. Her big eyes, her big ears, and her big teeth seemed strange.
5. The hunter was the hero because he saved Little Red Riding Hood and rescued Grandmother. He made sure that Little Red Riding Hood got home safely.

Page 91

In any order:
1. Don't talk to strangers. (mother)
2. Where are you going, little girl? (wolf)
3. I'm taking these to my grandmother. (girl)
4. Grandmother, what big teeth you have! (girl)
5. All the better to eat you, my dear. (wolf)

Page 92

1. Little Red Riding Hood
2. Mother
3. Grandmother
4. Grandmother
5. the wolf
6. Grandmother

Page 96

1. Goldilocks, Papa Bear, Mama Bear, and Baby Bear
2. Drawings should show a bowl of porridge, a chair, and a bed.
3. The things belonged to Baby Bear OR The things were always the third ones she looked at.
4. The bears put a new lock on the door so strangers couldn't come in while they were gone.
5. Answers will vary.

Page 97

Bowls should be correctly colored. Items drawn in the bowls must rhyme with the color words.

Fairy Tales & Folktales • EMC 756

Page 98

Answers will vary.

Page 102

1. Jack sold the cow.
2. Jack's mother was angry.
3. The beanstalk grew.
4. Jack climbed the beanstalk.
5. Jack knocked at the door.
6. Jack and his mother ate cheese.
7. Jack climbed the beanstalk.
8. The giant chased Jack.
9. Jack chopped down the beanstalk.
10. Jack and his mother bought food.

Page 103

yes—Jack tried to help his mother
   by selling the cow and
   climbing the beanstalk to look
   for food.
no—Jack would never have
   knocked on the giant's door if
   he had been shy.
yes—Jack went back to the giant's
   house even when he knew
   that the giant was dangerous.

yes—The woman gave Jack food
   and warned him about the
   giant.
no—She was generous because
   she gave Jack something
   each time he asked.

Page 104

Original sentences will vary.

1. Jack's stomach woke him up and
   reminded him to look for food.
2. They bought food with the coins in
   the giant's pockets.

Page 107

1. The lizard lived in the cave.
2. The ant moved in and made
   himself at home.
3. The ant answered as if he were
   a fierce and powerful animal.
4. The frog scared the ant out of the
   cave.
5. The cave made it seem louder
   because of the echo.
6. The sun was behind the frog and
   it made a big shadow.

Page 108

1. powerful
2. tramples
3. echoed
4. scurried
5. pounced

1. the tiger
2. the warthog and the lizard
3. the ant

Page 109

1. shadow
2. croak
3. echo
4. home

Hoe, window, boat, rose, bone,
doorknob, and bow should be
marked.

Page 110

Opposites—little, strong, quiet, go,
   answer, cry
Same meaning—huge, meek, noisy,
   halt, question, giggle
They all rhyme with the given words.

Drawings will vary.

Page 113

1. She wanted to touch the stars.
2. Her mother and father wouldn't
   help her.
3. She asked the pond and swam
   in it. She asked the fairies and
   danced with them. She followed
   the fairies' riddle and climbed a
   rainbow in the sky.
4. the pony
5. the girl
6. the fish
7. no
8. Answers will vary. Students should
   infer that the little girl was only
   dreaming.

Page 114

1. The little girl looked at stars outside
   her window.
2. The little girl danced with the
   fairies.
3. The little girl climbed the rainbow.
4. The little girl woke up on her
   bedroom floor.

Drawings will vary.

Page 115

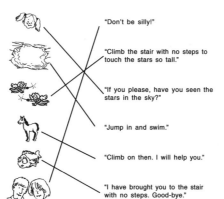

"Don't be silly!"

"Climb the stair with no steps to touch the stars so tall."

"If you please, have you seen the stars in the sky?"

"Jump in and swim."

"Climb on then. I will help you."

"I have brought you to the stair with no steps. Good-bye."

Page 116

1. swim, swam
2. dance, danced
3. climb, climbed
4. sent, send

Page 118

1. Two goats wanted to go across
   the bridge at the same time.
2. The goats pushed each other
   off the bridge and went home.

Original tales will vary.

Page 119

The goats are stubborn—Neither
wanted to give way.
Neither goat would go back. They
stood nose-to-nose for a long time.

The goats blame each other—
"Just see the trouble he caused."
Each muttered, "He is so stubborn."
They had accusing eyes.

Page 120

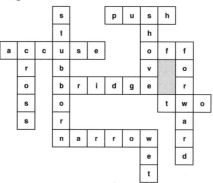

Page 121

1. queen   4. seen
2. green   5. teen
3. keen   6. screen

sunscreen
canteen
fourteen

Sentences will vary.

Page 125

Hansel left a trail of white pebbles.
Gretel trapped the witch in the oven.
Father was happy to see Hansel and
   Gretel.
Stepmother wanted to leave the
   children in the woods.
Witch wanted to eat a plump child.

Students' interpretations of the moral
will vary, but should include the idea
that Father, Hansel, and Gretel stuck
together even when they had little
money or food. They took care of
each other.

Page 126

yard, card, far
jar, star, carve

1. far
2. yard
3. card
4. jar
5. carve
6. star

Sentences will vary.

Page 127

One-syllable words—poor, starve,
   grabbed, plump, built
Two-syllable words—enough, outside,
   candy, pocket, finger, shining,
   asleep, children
Three-syllable words—woodcutter,
   stepmother

Page 131

1. a coin
2. some bread
3. the troll
4. 3
5. The poor man had helped him.
6. He sank to the bottom of the lake.
7. the troll
8. both the dwarf and the troll

Page 132

Dwarf, Troll, Poor Man, Dwarf, Troll,
Poor Man, Dwarf, Poor Man, Troll

Students' responses about their
favorite characters will vary.

Page 133

bare, spare
share, square
hare, scare

Drawings will vary.

Page 137

1. The garbage that the old man
   poured on the little man's house
   was called slops.
2. She peeled potatoes and tossed
   the peelings into the slop pail. She
   peeled carrots and tossed the
   peelings into the slop pail. She
   peeled onions and tossed the
   peelings into the slop pail. She
   washed dishes and poured the
   dirty water into the slop pail.
3. He carried it out the door and
   dumped it over the front wall.
4. The old man was dumping the
   slops on the little man's house.
5. They were good neighbors
   because they were considerate.
   They dumped their slops over
   the back wall once they
   discovered the little old man.

Page 138

There was a house with a wall all
   around it.
The wall is ten steps from the front
   door and ten steps from the back
   door.
On the other side of the front wall is
   a little house.

Students' drawings will vary.

Page 139

snail, pail
mail, trail

Students' drawings and sentences
will vary.

Other -ail words: bail, fail, hail, jail,
nail, quail, rail, sail, tail